STEAD:
THE MAN

STEAD: THE MAN

PERSONAL REMINISCENCES

EDITH K. HARPER

Introduction
MAJOR-GENERAL SIR
ALFRED E. TURNER, K.C.B., ETC.

White Crow

www.whitecrowbooks.com

Stead: The Man

Stead: The Man

First published in 1918 by William Rider & Son Ltd.
This copyright © 2025 by White Crow Productions Ltd. All rights reserved.
Published by White Crow Books, an imprint of White Crow Productions Ltd.

The right of the author has been asserted in accordance with
the Copyright, Design and Patents act 1988.

A CIP catalogue record for this book is available from the British Library.
For information, contact White Crow Books by e-mail: info@whitecrowbooks.com.

Cover Design by Astrid@Astridpaints.com
Interior design by Velin@Perseus-Design.com

Hardback: ISBN: 9781786772855
Paperback: ISBN: 9781786772862
eBook: ISBN: 9781786772879

Non-Fiction / BODY, MIND & SPIRIT / Spiritualism / Afterlife & Reincarnation

www.whitecrowbooks.com

Dedicated
To
"The Union of All who Love,
In the Service of All who Suffer."

CONTENTS

~

Introduction

BY MAJOR-GENERAL SIR
ALFRED E. TURNER, K.C.B., ETC., ETC.

~

A S A CLOSE AND INTIMATE friend of W.T. Stead, I have pleasure in writing an introduction to this work of Miss Edith Harper, whose long period of association with him gave her constant and unequalled opportunities of diving into the depths of the inner thoughts of that great thinker and single-minded philanthropist, whose mind was ever directed towards the betterment and improvement of the condition of his fellow-creatures, not only in this world but in preparation for the life beyond the border. He was absolutely fearless both physically and morally, and the "whips and scorns of time," and the taunts and ridicule which were hurled at him on account of his firm and unshaken belief in the continuity of life beyond the grave, and in the possibility of communicating with the spirits of those who have passed on, were to him as unworthy of serious attention as the "crackling of thorns under a pot."

I had no more valued friend than W.T. Stead, and his sudden and premature ending on the physical plane has caused a gap in my life that is hard indeed to fill, even though I and several other of his friends have been privileged to communicate with him spiritually on many occasions.

No man ever lived a more strenuous life, or one more devoted to the welfare of his fellow-creatures, and this perhaps led him to a too great indifference to his own mundane interests. His heart and his purse were ever open to those who came to him in difficulties and distress, for counsel and relief.

1

In this country of ours, probably impostors and blackmailers flourish under the aegis of the law more richly than in any other—and Stead was too generous, too open-hearted, too unsuspicious and too busy, to inquire closely into the circumstances of those who came to him for help. However, this one weakness in him, if it can so be called, only redounds to the credit of a generous and unsuspicious heart.

I venture to say that no one has ever been more fearless as to the so-called horrors of death, or more ready to meet it than W.T. Stead. It signified nothing to him but a phase, a step on that long upward path of evolution, which sooner or later we all must ascend till we reach that point where the secrets of nature and the mysteries of spirit-life will be made known to us, when we come into the presence of that great unknown Deity who, as Bacon wrote, "alone hath no beginning."

Stead was *the* man indeed, the typical man whom Browning must have had in his mind's eye when he wrote his beautiful lines:

"One who never turned his back, but marched breast forward,
Never doubted clouds would break,
Never dreamt, though right were worsted, wrong would triumph;
Held we fall to rise, are baffled to fight better;
Sleep to wake."

Miss Harper, by writing an account of some aspects of the life of a many-sided man, has earned the gratitude not only of Stead's countless friends, but of legions of thinking people, who feel that he had a mission to perform on earth, which he did not fail to accomplish in any respect. A perusal of *Stead: The Man*, coupled with one of *My Father*, by Miss Estelle Stead, will give as close an insight as can be obtained of the life and character of one of the best and most remarkable men of his time.

~ ALFRED E. TURNER.

Foreword

~

A S THIS VOLUME HAS NO pretensions to being a Biography but is only a sheaf of personal memories bound together with some details of W.T. Stead's psychic work more especially of the years wherein I was privileged to work with him which will supplement those already otherwise recorded, I make no attempt to sketch, even in outline, his enormous activities in the many other fields which lie white to the harvest of the biographer. However much many of his contemporaries may have disagreed with his views or his methods, posterity will find them to have been unanimous in agreement that the motive-power behind all his brilliant energies was of the highest and purest. So utterly unselfish, so full of the divine capacity to love and forgive, yet so infinitely human in his impetuous vehemence, in his fierce impassioned denunciation of all that is base and mean; at times an *enfant terrible*, making one hold one's breath in apprehension of the next *dénouement*, at others a St. Francis in modern garb, gathering up a stray wet kitten, storm-driven on the Embankment on a wintry night, and sheltering it tenderly under his coat; prince of journalists, apostle of peace, knight errant of womanhood, quixotic champion of forlorn hopes and struggling causes he has been truly called all these, and a full and complete record of his devoted life-work will be truly encyclopaedic when it arrives.

My best thanks are due to the executors of the late Mr. W.T. Stead for kindly allowing me to reproduce the frontispiece of the *Review of Reviews Memorial Number*, and certain copyright matter included in this book; to Miss Goodrich-Freer (Mrs. H. Spoer) for her contribution on "Borderland"; to Lady Archibald Campbell, Miss Lilian Whiting and

Miss Scatcherd for kindly sanctioning my quotations from their writings; to the editors of the *Contemporary Review*, the *Fortnightly Review*, *The Daily Mail*, *Light*, and the *Two Worlds*, for courteous permission to quote from Mr. Stead's articles and speeches; to Lady Warwick for her kindness in consenting to the publication of fuller details regarding the motor-car prophecy; to Mr. R. King for notes on Mr. Stead's horoscope; and to Mr. E. R. Serocold-Skeels for his kind help in revising the proofs. I also wish to record my gratitude to my publisher, the Honourable. Ralph Shirley (Messrs. Wm. Rider & Son, Ltd.), for his patience and consideration in the face of unforeseen difficulties.

EDITH K. HARPER.
The Apple Gate, Coombe Hill, S.W.

1

A House of Many Rooms

W.T. STEAD HAD A FAVOURITE saying, the inner meaning of which may be enlarged to any extent: "If I am remembered at all a hundred years hence, it will be as Julia's amanuensis!" To those who really knew him it is certain that the much beloved, much derided, much reviled "Julia's Bureau"—dearest to him of his many practical ideals for the benefit of humanity will ever stand as typical of the essential spirituality of all his activities. Like the burning-glass which concentrates the energy of the sun, it was the focus and outward manifestation of an altruism which sought expression in two worlds, the visible and the invisible.

Doubtless to a mind like his, intensely active and keenly analytical, the problem, "What? Whence? Whither?" early asserted itself, in spite of the rigid, Puritanical training of his childhood and youth. His writings reveal the eager soul that was constantly looking from the earth to the stars and scanning with inquiring yet reverent eyes the marvellous intertwining of spiritual with physical things.

He often declared he was born "without the bump of veneration"; but he only meant that he could not always adopt what Matthew Arnold called "stock ideas." He must needs learn, think, explore for himself, and if at times he startled the world with the result of such exploration, he took it as all in the day's work and said, "You cannot judge of the impact you have made till you see the force of the reaction it sets up!"

He was of a type that is mentally and physically fearless, having the Pilgrim Fathers for its spiritual ancestry and finding in Oliver Cromwell the embodiment of its political and religious ideals. Perhaps, too, he had inherited the spirit of the warlike Scandinavians from whom he claimed far-back descent.[1] Carlyle finds in the essence of the Scandinavian mythology, more than in any other, "a recognition of the divineness of Nature; sincere communion of man with the mysterious, invisible Powers visibly seen at work in the world around him." From those "hardy Norsemen" one could imagine came the leonine head and the brilliant sea-blue eyes. There were again times when he suggested, rather, some inspired patriarch or law-giver of old, some warrior-prophet filled with the sacred fire of Sinai.

From his own vivid picture of his early surroundings and education, in the restricted yet loving atmosphere of the Northumberland manse into which he was born,[2] where "plain living and high thinking" were the rule of life, we learn that he was taught by his father, the minister, to reason vigorously for himself, and to express his thoughts in "vehement polemic" at the family breakfast-table. Doubtless in those early days of mental sword-crossing he acquired his inimitable readiness and fluency in debate. "His thoughts were like lightning and clothed themselves at once in words." This description—Dean Milman's—of the oratory of Lord Macaulay, might well have been written of W.T. Stead. Such a whirlwind of utterance was sometimes in after years the despair of those who had to report his public speeches, and he was greatly amused when on one occasion the pressmen sent up, beforehand, a note to the

---

[1] Mr. Stead told me that according to tradition his family was of Swedish origin and settled in England during the reign of Queen Elizabeth. E. K. H.

[2] He was born on July 5, 1849, at Embleton Manse, near Alnwick. The exact hour of his birth is uncertain, but those who are learned in the lore of the stars will read with interest these approximate notes on his nativity, kindly sent to me by Mr. Robert King.

"W.T. Stead was born under the influence of the regal sign Leo, his ruler is therefore the Sun, which on the day of his birth was in the maternal sign Cancer. At his death the Moon was in the ninth house of the map (the house that rules long journeys), in conjunction with the malefic planet Uranus whose influence is always sudden or unexpected.

"His Leo nature, tempered by this Cancer Sun, would give him his large, glowing, dominant temperament, and yet always subordinated to the loving 'motheringness' which was so truly a feature of his personality."

platform asking if "Mr. Stead could kindly manage to speak at less than the rate of a thousand words a minute!"

He was most felicitous when conversing with those whom personally he liked, and with whom he had much inner sympathy, while differing greatly from them on certain crucial points, on which both felt equally strongly. He would carry on the war of words to its utmost limits, following out some quaintly original and tantalizingly unanswerable line of logic, and mercilessly laying bare any weak spots in his antagonist's armour, but preserving throughout his own unruffled good-humour.

Occasionally, when he was very much "rushed," on going-to-press days, for instance, when his copy was being clamoured for by the printers, and some uncomprehending stranger, who had gained an always-ready access to the sanctum, did not realize it was "time to go," I have known him suddenly cut short a discussion which threatened to become endless and had ceased to interest him, by putting both hands on the visitor's shoulders, with an indulgent smile, and playfully running him to the door, with the parting benediction: "I think you are quite wrong, my dear sir! But come back and talk it over with me another time."

Though a North-countryman might be reluctant to admit it, the people of the "remote and savage North," in spite of their hard-headedness, are near enough to the Scottish border to feel at least a distant kinship with those to whom seership is a gift of long inheritance. No doubt as a child he early became aware of the eeriness of the Threshold; and we can imagine how he sat in the ingle-nook on winter nights, listening, wide-eyed, to the creepsome tales of Wellington Mill, a famous haunted house in the neighbourhood, within a mile of which he spent his boyish days. "My father's deacon," he relates,[3] "Mr. Edward Elliott, one of the most excellent and sober-minded of men," was tenant of the Mill, "and the stories of the hauntings were familiar to me from my childhood."

He speaks too of the feeling of awe with which, as a boy, he once found himself alone in the haunted Mill, though he "saw nothing and heard nothing." Through life he was, as he always said, "in blinkers" so far as clairvoyance was concerned. He neither "heard" nor "saw," and the earlier years of his life are curiously void of psychic happenings with the solitary exception of one decidedly weird experience that befell him as a youth, at Hermitage castle, near Liddesdale, when spending a holiday in Scotland.[4]

---

[3] *Real Ghost Stories.*

[4] Ibid.

When it is remembered that had these powers been evolved in him as fully as was his undoubted gift of prevision and the receiving of "impressions," one sees that he would perhaps have been too deeply enthralled by the wonders of the "Fourth Dimension" to have achieved his painful conquests of the dark things of this world.

None but those born into the atmosphere of the ingle-nook, as he was, can ever quite understand the unforgettable associations it conveys; a thought of comfort, of deep family affection, of "sweet household talk," and fireside dreamings which can never be expressed in words. It is the quintessence of Home, another name whose thousand unutterable meanings are found in the speech of no other land. And because the spirit of the home-love was in his blood he longed to make the whole world one great ingle-nook, with none left shivering, outcast, in the cold. Warming "both hands at the fire of life" he longed to draw all friendless hands into his kind human clasp, so that they too might feel the glow.

He had an ingenious theory that the human Ego is like a man who lives in a house of many stories and many rooms. The indwelling spirit, or Master of the House, inhabits the different rooms at different times, according to the calls made upon him from the outer world. When dissatisfied with some of his own writings he sometimes remarked, "That was written by the part of me which lives on the basement and haggles at the door!" Again, when his magic pen had expressed some especially felicitous saying, he would observe, with a smile: "I suppose that is the part of me that lives on the top floor!" He delighted to dilate on this and many another quaint conceit that took his fancy, applying it all round. Of an unkind action, or an uncharitable criticism, his brief comment: "It's pretty clear that that man only lives on his ground floor!" implied also the serene conviction that the misguided person would sooner or later begin to climb upstairs. It was his firm belief, in following out his metaphor, that in this "dwellinghouse "of every individual exists also a top-story beautiful to behold, illumined by eternal sunlight and opening to the unknown splendours of the Infinite Beyond.

He seemed as though perpetually sustained by some unfailing source of energy that hurled him headlong through existence, as on some great Adventure. This he expressed as being "switched on to the Power-House of the Universe," and he maintained that it was "up to everyone" to be thus switched up simply by keeping the line of communication prayer open and in good working order every day. To him the faith of a little child came absolutely naturally, but when the uncomprehending called him "credulous" in the matter of his Spiritualistic beliefs he merely quoted oracularly Cecil Rhodes's dictum: "There's a fifty percent, chance, either way. Make your choice. Only don't *hedge*!" And he took his own chance all his life long "on the side of the angels," saying:

"I have gone doubles or quits on the Senior Partner all my days. He has never failed me, and I don't think He ever will."

The "Senior Partner" was his favourite term for God. He always held that it was no use sitting down and expecting Providence to do a man's work for him. We must first seek earnestly for "signposts," and having found them we must "go ahead" with all our might, asking God to be our Senior Partner and realizing that He will expect us to carry out our full share of the undertaking. Sometimes, he admitted good-humouredly, he made the mistake of trying to take too large a share of the business on to his own shoulders, and he quoted many a good story against himself, apropos, such as, for instance his father's dry query, "Aren't you going to leave a little for the Lord Himself to do, William?"

But those who knew him best can recall how in some long-drawn-out tangle of perplexity, when light seemed for the moment withdrawn, there were "lions in the path," and in the press of conflict it would seem that the Guiding Will had been strangely inexorable, even strangely hard, how those clear, far-seeing blue eyes—which saw so deeply and so tenderly into the problems and mysteries of existence—would look for just a moment, with a quick, half-puzzled second glance, as though to be quite sure of having grasped the stern significance aright; then the old calm serenity would return, the loving trust, the unquenchable faith—nay, the *certainty* that "His 'best' is better for us than our own can ever be," and that to belong to the Great All-Wise, All-Loving Father, just to be used by Him as a humble instrument for His own inscrutable purposes, is the only possible rule of life. There is no describing the effect of seeing this constant attitude of sweet, unshakable trust, lived out daily before one's eyes, in the midst of the most pressing of the world's affairs. To many it was the most lovable, the most touching trait in his character.

The natural outcome of his constant sense of the Fatherhood of God was his no less constant sense of human brotherhood, not as defined by modern Socialism but as expressed in Russell Lowell's ideal of a civic Church whose scope—as Mazzini defined it—should be "great as the Love of God, wide as the needs of Man." He would never label himself Socialist however, except in the sense of "an equal fellowship of Duty." Sometimes he laughingly declared, "Yes, I am in favour of Socialism, *plus* common-sense and the ten commandments; but as the Socialism of the present day is conspicuously lacking in the one, and jumps violently with hobnailed boots upon the other, I am not a Socialist!" He defined his Imperialism in the same way, always "plus common-sense and the ten commandments." His ideal of Social Service was based on no cast-iron organization of sects' and parties, but was simply "the union of all who love in the service of to all who suffer," for he felt in his soul the unspeakable kinship of all humanity in its struggle towards the light:

"My brother kneels, so saith Kabir,
To stone and brass, in heathen wise.
But in my brother's soul I hear
My own unanswered agonies.
His God is as his fates assign;
His prayer is all the world's and mine."[5]

Like his hero Cromwell he made the Bible his mainstay; it was to him as a "well of living waters," to which he turned constantly for help and guidance, never failing to find there what he sought. His favourite verse was:

"Trust in the Lord with all thy heart. Lean not unto thine own understanding. In all thy ways acknowledge Him and He shall direct thy path."

He used to say that these words were imprinted on his mind before he was sixteen, and were probably largely answerable for his lack of confidence in his capacity to steer his own course. "In the atmosphere of these verses I have spent my life. I believe that some power—not ourselves—is actively concerned in making the best of us, and that this Invisible Intelligence can make the most of us if we combine the mental attitude of absolute readiness to obey the word of command with a passionate determination to do whatever is given us to do with our utmost strength and skill." This, in substance, I once heard him say to an American visitor, a lady, who had called at his office to ask, among other questions, if Mr. Stead "believed in a God"? ...

"Good Heavens!" he exclaimed, when the visitor had departed, "Surely I have shouted my beliefs from the house-tops long enough!"

Visitors to the "Sanctum" at Mowbray House must often have noticed the words of that text inscribed upon the left-hand panel of

---

[5] "The Prayer," Rudyard Kipling.

the door. On the right-hand panel was the Eastern saying: "Seek not thy Fate: thy Fate is seeking thee!" while above both were scrolled the words "Attempt great things for God; expect great things from God." On the outside of the second door of the Sanctum hung a little framed picture of "Silence," a hooded face, with finger on lip.

If he were disappointed or cast down he often cheered himself by reading the most joyous of the Psalms. Like Carlyle he held them to be "the truest emblem of a man's moral progress and warfare here below."[6]

In common with John Ruskin, he quoted copiously from the Bible in his writings, giving his quotations the most unlooked-for yet entirely apt significance, and one of the most charming examples of his gift of writing for children is to be found in *The Bairns' Bible: a Talk about the Old Book*, one of the familiar series of Books for the Bairns which he began in and which have found their way to children all over the world.

"Every person makes his own Bible," he once quaintly wrote.

> "Each one selects parts that suit him and that speak to him. ... It is better to get one text well into your mind and into your life than it is to wander over all the chapters without making any use of them."

Perhaps the secret of his kinship with children lay in his own childlike heart, where dwelt the spirit of Peter Pan, the boy who wouldn't grow up. Everything interested, touched, or amused him. He wanted to share his treasures with everyone. When he encountered giants everyone must come and listen to the fearsome tale. It was sometimes said that he had no sense of humour. For banalities no, he had not. But for sheer joyous elfin fun, or subtle keen-edged wit, he had a vast relish. A smart repartee delighted him, even when he felt compelled in duty bound to shake his head and let the smile disappear into his beard.

The Doxology was another of his favourite ways of shouting "Hurrah" to the universe. Once, when the connection between the Doxology and the event was not very obvious to the ordinary understanding, he said in answer to a mild protest that the hymn was not appropriate to the occasion:—"Not appropriate? Of course it's appropriate! Don't you know all things work for the best! If it's anything good sing the Doxology. If its anything bad *sing it twice*!"

He was "caught out" once, however, when the news came in the summer of 1911 that the Italians had seized Tripoli. Happening to hear

---

[6] "On Heroes."

him declare himself forcibly on the subject of "international highway robbery." I could not refrain from asking if he did not wish to sing the Doxology?" No, I don't!" he roared. "I want to open the office-window and shout, "Damn! Damn! Damn!" to all the people in the street!"

He confessed frankly to having "no ear for music." I remember his saying, apropos of a book he was sending me to review: "It is full of your music delirium—an unknown language to me!" Yet his sense of "rhythm" was absolutely perfect, and I have noticed that certain harmonies did really attract him, the stately chords of Luther's hymn, "Ein Feste Burg," for instance, and the deep devotion of Schubert's "Ave Maria." In curious contrast to these, he liked the rollicking strains of "Weel may the keel row!"[7] for it brought back memories of his youth. ... No matter how tired and overdriven he might be when he came down to Cambridge House for the weekly meeting of "Julia's Circle" the small group of friends who met every Wednesday night, he never failed to find renewed strength by joining vigorously in the singing of the hymn with which the sitting opened.

"Hymns," he once wrote, "Often help us like angels and ministers of grace, and disappear again into the void." He had a most boundless beautiful faith in their power to give comfort and solace in all times of need. Well indeed can we realize his asking those splendid bandsmen of the *Titanic* to play, in the last dark hour, "Nearer my God to Thee." I have known him, after a hard day's work at his office, go and spend the greater part of a long night with a sick man to whom the usual ministrations had proved unavailing in soothing the delirium of fever. Patiently Mr. Stead sat by the bedside holding the hot hand, then, all at once, as though moved by some sudden inspiration, he began softly to sing the familiar old hymn "I have a Father in the Promised Land." Verse after verse he sang, with its stirring refrain, till at length sleep closed the tired eyelids, and our Chief[8] stole silently from the room, looking utterly weary but supremely triumphant.

Recollections such as these come thronging back to memory and might be multiplied a hundred-fold, yes, many times a hundred-fold. They are but a few passing glimpses, through different windows, of the radiant Ego which for nearly three-and-sixty years of earth-life inhabited the House called W.T. Stead.

---

[7] A Tyne-side folk-song, as familiar to North-country people as "God Save the King."

[8] To his staff, and to the members of 'sJulia's circle, he was always ""the Chief."

2

"The Beginnings of Seership"

~

O N AN EVENING IN 1911, at one of the weekly meetings of the
Circle at Cambridge House, Wimbledon, not many months
before that unique group of kindred spirits met for the last
time, Mr. Stead brought down with him to the sitting a venerable
journalist, a stranger to most of the company, whom he presented to
us as "the very first person to interest me in Spiritualism when I was
at Darlington more than thirty years ago."

Naturally the new-comer was a source of much interest to us all, and
I remember vaguely wondering, as I sat in the Circle taking notes at
the Chief's elbow and trying to keep pace with his flying pen, whether
it was pure chance that had led to the mention of the subject between
them on the eve of Mr. Stead's severing his journalistic connection
with the North in 1880, or whether the moment had been chosen by
Destiny for that special and particular purpose. All things have their
cause and their beginning, and, as the Chief remarked meditatively: "It
is curious to think that that passing conversation with a north-country
pressman was apparently the first link in the long chain that had led
up to Julia's Bureau."

In his youthful village days at Howden-on-Tyne, no whisper from
the Invisibles seems to have reached his conscious ear. Sensitive and
highly-strung, his boyish feelings apparently found sufficient outlet in his
ardent devotion to his mother and the fervent outpourings of emotional

13

religion. But of the "Sixth Sense" he had in himself no conscious awareness, nor are any stories on record even of such precocious developments as abound in the *Anecdotes of Pious Children*. He neither spoke Hebrew at the age of three, nor translated the Scriptures at the age of six, as is related of some of those unfortunate babies who generally seem to have died young, nor did "shades of the prison-house" becloud and dim the finer, subtler sense wherein Wordsworth finds our pre-natal kinship with God. On the contrary, as one follows his life-story there is a visible developing of the spiritual consciousness, Matthew Arnold would have called it a dawning of Hellenism, though it continued to express itself in Hebraic form. One seems to feel the beating of the wings of his soul in its struggles to free itself from the trammels of the atmosphere into which he was born.

He said he always had a hyper-sensitive imagination and often told how he had tortured himself when a very small boy by dismal wonderings as to what would become of him if his parents were suddenly to die! His next great tribulation was a fearful misgiving lest he should never find favour in the eyes of a girl, because of his un-likeness to the other boys of the village. In fact, as he often laughingly remarked, when speaking of those long-past apprehensions byway of admonition against the evil of meeting difficulties half-way, "The very worst troubles in my life have always been the things that *never happened!*"

Nevertheless, he admitted to being still an adept in the art of self-torture, while he deprecated it as one of the deadliest of every-day sins. Once when I was in much anxiety over the illness of a friend, who had been pronounced by six doctors in consultation to be suffering from an incurable affection of the heart though a seventh took a different view, he wrote me a letter so characteristic in its note of resolute hopefulness, that it may well be quoted here. It is dated November 21, 1909, and was written from Hayling Island:

> Do not grieve so much over. In the first place there is one chance in seven that he is not suffering from what the six doctors say, and one chance in seven is more than many of us have. Next, it is illogical to argue that because the father died in this way the son must die also in the same way. Thirdly, it is usually people who have weak hearts who live longest; old Holyoake who lived to be eighty odd told me that the secret of his longevity was that he was such a weakling he always had to avoid taking risks. Fourthly, granting the worst and that your friend is stricken with an incurable and deadly disease, wherein does that

differ from you and me? We all suffer from the incurable deadly disease of mortality. Every day brings you and me nearer the grave, and it is at least possible that both you and I may get there before him. Don't dwell on the dark side of the case. Remember nothing ever happens that is not ordered in love, and that nine-tenths of our troubles are self-created to torment us before the real trouble comes. Don't think that I am unsympathetic. I am not. I am arguing against one of my own besetting sins, and you need the argument even more than sympathy. Besides, you do not know what precious jewels this adversity, ugly and venomous as it seems, may yet carry, like the fabled toad, in its head. Cheer up. Rejoice! It is not what we expect that happens, and remember that come health, come death, He doeth all things well. ...

Now, cheer up. Be joyful in God and Rejoice. Don't take these things lying down. But up, confront the universe of love with a glad heart!

As later events proved, his optimism was fully justified, for in this curious case the verdict of the seventh doctor eventually proved right, and that of the six others absolutely wrong. "Difficulties are the polishing-stones of one's life," was another of his bits of crystallized wisdom, and "In the eyes of Almighty Love nothing is great, nothing is small."

In the brilliant decade of the 'eighties, when he forced home "The Truth about the Navy," revealing the weak links in our coast defence,[9] when statesmen and cabinet ministers danced to his piping, and it might indeed have been said of him as of Henry V,

> "Turn him to any cause of policy,
> The gordian knot of it he will unloose."

the clear vision of the Belgian savant Emile de Laveleye discerned the sacred fire that glowed deep down beneath those furious activities. "*Il est reveur, mystique, presque spirite!*" de Laveleye wrote of him in 1885, when the Maiden Tribute Agitation was at its height.

Through the intuitions of his own soul he received what he called his "signposts." Once he clearly saw a signpost he steered his course

---

[9] He coined his famous phrase, "Two Keels to One," about 1907. "Good sense and good English could not be better united," said Mr. J. L. Garvin in his memorial tribute.

by that alone, and by no other chart whatever. "Souls are naturally endowed with the gift of pre-vision," said Plutarch. This is true of W.T. Stead. In three instances at least did he receive a definite, unmistakable "warning" of what was about to happen in the near future. The first was in 1880, while he was still editing the *Northern Echo* at Darlington, the first English provincial town to raise its voice in "passionate protest" against the Bulgarian Atrocities of 1876. He has told the story many a time and oft; how, on New Year's Day, 1880, he was seized by the sudden conviction that he would have to leave Darlington and take up work on the London press in the course of that year, though he "knew of absolutely no London paper that would have him on its staff." He told a friend the same day of his premonition, and receiving a sceptical but friendly warning to do "nothing rash" on the strength of so vague a security, characteristically retorted that he intended to do nothing at all. The "call "would come to him, he averred, and that in the course of the year! Nothing seemed more unlikely; yet his presentiment came absolutely true. By the law of "the unexpected" the *Pall Mall Gazette*, then one of the most violently pro-Turk of all the London papers, changed its proprietor, its principles, and its editor, with the change of Ministry. W.T. Stead, then as always "a good Russian" was offered the post of assistant-editor to Mr. (now Lord) Morley, and left Darlington in the September of 1880, exactly as his vision had foretold, and that even though he had renewed his contract with the proprietor of the Echo a few months previously, a claim which the latter kindly but naturally waived.

His second and third premonitions were equally spontaneous and noteworthy. The former occurred while he was on a holiday in the Isle of Wight in 1883, "when the great troopers which had just brought back Lord Wolseley's army from the first Egyptian campaign were lying in the Solent." While out of doors one day he suddenly heard as it were a voice within himself telling him to "look sharp and make ready," as he would have to take full control of the *P.M.G.* before a certain date in the March of the following year. He felt startled, as he was sure that this was a "warning" that his Chief, Morley, was doomed to die. On his return to London he lost no time in making known his "presentiment" to all whom it might concern, though naturally not acquainting them with the gloomy construction he had at first put upon it, for the idea was subsequently suggested that Mr. Morley would enter Parliament. He was only laughed at for his pains, however; no one scouted the notion of entering Parliament more strenuously than did Mr. Morley himself.

But again the unexpected happened. The prophecy was fulfilled to the date and to the letter. Mr. Ashton Dilke, then Member for Newcastle-on-Tyne, suddenly became dangerously ill. Mr. Morley was selected as Liberal candidate in his place, and was duly returned to Parliament in the following March, on which the full control of the *Pall Mall Gazette* passed into Mr. Stead's hands.

His third presentiment occurred later still. It came to him in 1885, towards the end of the Maiden Tribute trial. He felt a sudden certainty that he would be sent to gaol for two months, and this while those "who considered themselves most in a position to speak with authority" were confident in their belief that he would not be sent to gaol at all.

When the judge passed sentence of three months' imprisonment, Mr. Stead relates that it was all he could do to refrain from protesting that his Lordship was surely mistaken and had intended to say "two months." But great was his excitement when, later, on entering his cell, he looked at the card on the door, bearing his name and sentence and saw that the actual duration of the latter counted from the beginning of the trial. As the hearing had lasted nearly a month there remained therefore only two months and seven days of his sentence to run. And thus his third presentiment was fulfilled.

After that, for a season, the voice of prophecy seems to have become dumb. Yet there runs through many of his writings a curious persistent note of bodeful coincidence, if one may so term it, when read by the light of the event which closed his earthly career. "Foreseeing" is too strong a description in this instance, yet the following words from the preface to *Hymns that have Helped* bear an application full of pathos. He is writing of the reluctance of most people to "testify as to their experiences in the deeper matters of the soul," a reluctance with which be it said, he had not the slightest sympathy, and which he caustically described as "an inverted egotism, selfishness masquerading in the guise of reluctance to speak of self. ... Wanderers across the wilderness of Life" he goes on, "ought not to be chary of telling their fellow travellers where they found the green oasis, the healing spring, or the shadow of a great rock in a desert land. It is not regarded as egotism *when the passing steamer signals across the Atlantic wave news of her escape from perils of iceberg or fog.*" Alas for the days to be, when the heart of humanity would wait, sick with hope deferred, for "news of escape from peril of iceberg," and for tidings of good cheer that never came.

One finds yet another of those strangely fateful coincidences of which his life and his writings are so full, on looking back to the Christmas

Number of the *Review of Reviews* for 1893, which consisted of a story by Mr. Stead himself, entitled *From the Old World to the New*, pure fiction at the time it was written, yet destined to be singularly fulfilled by fact in after years. He dwelt at great length in this tale on the dangers of icebergs in the Atlantic Ocean, and actually laid his *mise-en-scene* on board the White Star Liner *Majestic*, giving in addition a portrait of her commander, Captain Smith, the same Captain Smith who, twenty-one years later was to sink with the "unsinkable" *Titanic*. In the narrative he imagines the Majestic steering her way through a dense fog, which suddenly lifts, revealing "a dazzling array of icebergs, ever shifting and moving" near the vessel. A psychic touch finds its way into the story in the episode of the discovery, through telepathy, of some shipwrecked persons on one of the icebergs, and a note of singular pathos and prophecy echoes from Mr. Stead's words:

"The ocean-bed in the run of the liners is strewn with the whitening bones of thousands who have taken their passage ... but who never saw their destination!"

In 1909, in a speech which he delivered to the Members of the Cosmos Club, Chandos Street, W.C., in describing what he felt to be the barriers interposed by the Society for Psychical Research against communications from the Beyond, he drew a graphic, imaginary picture of himself, shipwrecked and drowning in the sea, and calling frantically for help. "Suppose that instead of throwing me a rope the rescuers should shout back, 'Who are you? What is your name?' 'I am Stead! W.T. Stead! I am drowning here in the sea! Throw me the rope. Be quick!' But instead of throwing me the rope they continue to shout back, 'How do we know you are Stead? Where were you born? Tell us the name of your grandmother!' Well, that is pretty typical of the 'help' given by the S.P.R. to the friends who are trying to make us hear them from the Other Side!"

During the few minutes allowed for questions and debate after the lecture, a lady in the audience, evidently puzzled by Mr. Stead's frequent reference to his son in the present tense, "Willie told me yesterday"—"Willie is going with me tomorrow," and so on, asked tentatively: "Is your son alive, Mr. Stead?"

The Chief was round in a flash, in the lady's direction. "Alive?" he called, in his ringing voice. "Of course he is! He died just two years ago. He is more alive than ever!"

That brief sentence sums up his whole attitude of mind towards death.

3

My First Meeting with W.T. Stead

⌒

THE BEGINNING OF MY PERSONAL friendship with W.T. Stead dates back to my early girlhood, twenty-three years ago, when my home was in the north of England. My constant working life with him began in 1907, when, on my taking up residence in London, he offered me secretarial work in connection with his book *The M.P. for Russia*, to which I shall refer later. From that time onward I was a member of his staff, acting later as his assistant in connection with his psychic work, more particularly "Julia's Bureau," likewise being custodian of what he called his "Archives," also his private correspondence and documents, and his literary and journalistic articles, which were in my charge at Cambridge House—almost the only place where there was room enough for such a vast collection, for it was his invariable rule to "keep everything." He almost never destroyed a letter, and the most apparently trivial note or newspaper cutting he liked carefully filed, for as he said "You never know what use it may be, nor of what it may form the connecting link." In the case of any important document he always demanded three and even four copies, and the rapidly accumulating mass of material thus acquired was the despair of his secretaries and helpers. What was to become of it all, and where was it to be put when it overflowed all storage bounds! None but those who worked with him day by day can understand the indescribable feeling almost of stupefaction that overcame us when suddenly, "in the twinkling of an eye," the end came, and that furious

19

output was instantly stilled. ... Even yet, thinking of these things, it is hard to realize, difficult to understand.

It was part of my work for him, in the intervals of other things, to arrange this voluminous mass of material in datal order. He had some idea of having it all in readiness for his immediate use when necessary, under the different headings "Psychic," "Political," "Peace," "Ethical and Religious," and so forth. Each section, with its various subsections, contained material for a separate memoir in itself. Under no one heading could justice be done to his superb ideals, the magnitude of his work, nor the totality of his many-faceted nature.

"You must write the psychic part," he said to me, only a few days before he sailed on the last, long journey. I said jokingly, "I had better begin at once, so that you may correct the proofs!" But now I feel my pen, though quickened with measureless sympathy and affection, all too inadequate to convey a tithe of that immense labour of love strongest of all the cords of service that bound him

"To the world's sad heart."

Yet, if the several pens of those who together shared his deepest aspirations, record such memories of him as came within their scope of intimate personal knowledge, then someday, perchance, some master hand may fitly weave together the different threads, so that the beautiful pattern of his life shall stand out, bright and fair, for future eyes.

How vividly I recall my first meeting with W.T. Stead. A picture radiant with "the moonlight of memory," it glows from the background of an autumn day in the early nineties. He had ceased, the previous year, to edit the *Pall Mall Gazette* and had founded the *Review of Reviews*.[10]

He was on one of his rare, flying visits to the North of England, when a relative of his, who was also an acquaintance of our own, invited my mother and me to take tea at her house in Newcastle, to meet Mr. Stead."

A little perhaps to my disappointment, as I must admit, when the day arrived, and we with it, there were several other guests, both men and women. With the pardonable instinct of youth for monopoly I suppose I had looked forward to having him "all to myself" for a long talk, for my mind was full of the myriad questions I was longing to ask him. But when we entered the room, there he was, seated at one side of a long tea-table,

---

[10] Mr. Stead founded the Review of Reviews in 1890. Mr., afterwards Sir, George Newnes, co-operated with him in the publication of the first three numbers.

in a big easy-chair, surrounded by a bevy of admirers, one of whom, a rather elderly lady who seemed extremely deaf, was holding a large ear-trumpet into which Mr. Stead was speaking with animation. He had already made one long speech at a meeting in the afternoon, and was to address a second meeting in the evening, on his favourite subject, "The Civic Church," his ideal from the days when, as a youth going home from work, he used to look from the Manors Station over "the house-crowded valley" in the shadow of All Saints' Church, Newcastle, and shudder over the barriers that separated human hearts. I remember sitting studying the mobile face, with the bushy dark hair and beard, and the vivid luminous blue eyes, and thinking that he reminded me somehow of quicksilver. An ocean of white tablecloth interspersed with islands of the delicious cakes of the hospitable North, separated me from him. Suddenly he seemed to become aware of my gaze fixed I hope not too resentfully upon the monopolizing ear-trumpet, and perhaps some telepathic message flashed from my insistent mind to his, for he suddenly jumped up from his easy-chair and, coming round the table to where I sat, took hold of both my hands and exclaimed, with one of those searching glances of his which seemed to penetrate one's whole being like a lightning-flash—

"Why, my dear little girl! Why did you not come and speak to me!"

Then we talked. Or rather, he talked and the rest of us listened. I remember how, even then, as a young girl, I felt the extraordinary power of his personality. His mind, the soul within him, the real man, seemed to leap beyond all "bounds of time and space" with a kind of imperious yet appealing *insouciance* that swept all before it, like some headlong torrent. One felt, in listening to him, "You see mentally far beyond anything you can say. You utter the thoughts of another world, careless of the words in which you embody them."

Someone mentioned the theatre, and I recall his saying that he had never been inside the doors of a theatre in his life. "I am going someday," he added, with an anticipatory smile, "when I have time. ... But it is such a big thing, I feel I should throw myself into it headlong, so for the present I'd better stay outside!"[11]

---

[11] Many years later he witnessed his "first play"—"The Tempest"—at His Majesty's Theatre, and entered with keen zest and enjoyment into its beauties, and its psychic setting. His sense of dramatic effect made him an excellent critic. After that he continued from time to time to visit the theatre, though he did not always see eye to eye with some of the managers about some of their productions, and, as usual, expressed himself on the subject vigorously and picturesquely.

An hour or two later, when my mother and I had to leave to catch our train, he said he and his son Willie who was there with him would accompany us to the station. I recall Willie that day as a slim boy of about seventeen, somewhat shy, yet with a remarkable dignity of bearing, who acted as his father's secretary and seemed to worship the ground he walked on. So off we all started, into the murky November night, "Willie" escorting my mother, and Mr. Stead's arm thrust through mine in characteristic fashion as we walked through the crowds, down Westgate Hill, he talking unceasingly in that charming, flattering way he had which seemed to assume that the mind of the listener saw equally with his, the breadth and height and depth of his own unfettered outlook. He talked of his own early days in the Quayside office; of *Real Ghost Stories* then in course of preparation had I any occult experiences? if any came my way, send them along; *Real Ghost Stories* was to appear in December as a Christmas Number. The Journal of Marie Bashkirtseff—as the Book of the Month, was it not a "human document, with a vengeance!"—what did I think of it, and of her? This led on to Russia, Tolstoy, Siberia, and his own imprisonment the—"red-letter day" of his life, he called it, and so on, and so on, he kept the brilliant ball a-rolling until we reached the Central station, where my last recollection of him is as he stood with "Willie" by the railway-carriage window, bidding me come and see him in London, and calling "God bless you!" with a wave of his hand, as the train began to move.

Some months before that episode, in the same year, I had been one of the competitors in an Examination for a Scholarship in Contemporary History, which Mr. Stead had inaugurated in connection with the *Review of Reviews*. The value of the Scholarship was £300, tenable for three years, the successful candidate to reside for a year at a time in France, Germany, and Russia respectively, for the purpose of studying the language and literature of these countries. The Competition was open to women of any age up to thirty, and residents of any part of Great Britain and the Colonies were eligible to compete. The examination papers consisted of questions set from Mr. Stead's Character-sketches and articles on the Progress of the World which had appeared in the Review of: Reviews during the previous six months, and as may be imagined these covered a rather extensive ground in relation to British and Foreign men and affairs. The notice of the Competition, in the *Review of Reviews*, particularly attracted my attention at a time when I was in deep grief over the death of my father, an event which had robbed me of the dearest of friends and confidants. Steeped as he was in the philosophy of Carlyle, and the new-world Platonism of Ralph Waldo Emerson, it was easy for me to find a latent kinship between my father's mind and that which had launched forth the Jovian thunderbolts of the *Pall Mall Gazette*. And though I did not then understand the full extent of conscious communion, yet I had a curious feeling that my father himself was urging me not to give way to hopeless grief and brooding, but to be "up and doing," and continue to develop my mind by reading and study. So by way of absorbing myself in something useful, I threw myself heart and soul into reading hard at the *Review of Reviews*, though I had not the slightest hope of winning the scholarship, which, as a matter of fact, was ultimately "tied "between two ladies, one or both of whom had reached the age-limit. I did, however, come out fourth on the list, and it was a delightful surprise when, a few days after my memorable meeting with Mr. Stead, I received a letter from him, enclosing a cheque for ten guineas, of which he wrote: "I have pleasure in asking your acceptance; it is awarded to you in connection with the Contemporary History Scholarship. You are the highest of all those under twenty." Then he added some kind words of congratulation and encouragement, saying in conclusion (which gave me even more satisfaction than the cheque), "I remember with pleasure the opportunity I had of meeting you when I was at Newcastle."

What endless stories could be told of his kind and graceful acts of encouragement to young beginners—pilgrims on the thorny Way of literature, and Life.

It was many years, however, before I was able to fulfil my promise to "go and see him in London." Family and domestic affairs conspired to keep me in the North, and though I had kind and friendly letters from Mr. Stead from time to time, and continued to follow the Progress of the World through his eyes, mirrored in the *Review of Reviews*, yet long years passed before I found myself once again face to face with him, in response to his oft-repeated invitation. This time we met in his own sanctum at Mowbray House, that famous spot memorable in so many lives, which stands at the corner of Norfolk Street, between the river and the busy Strand. It was in 1906, again an autumn day. The dark hair and beard had turned iron-grey, almost white, and he looked bigger and burlier than I remembered him, but the ringing voice, the hearty infectious laugh, above all the wonderful blue eyes, were just the same. So was the curious, familiar sense most people felt when talking to him, of having known him, and he them, always.

I remember that among other things he talked that day about a series of books he contemplated issuing—*Sagas of the English*—for young readers, in the shape of stories based upon stirring events in the history of our own country. We argued a little about the treatment of these stories. He insisted that they must be "bluggy," instancing the delight of "Helen's Babies" in the gruesome fate of the Giant Goliath, and his own early "thrills" over the lurid and ferocious. I suggested appealing rather to the sense of beauty supposed to be latent in all children, and with that he agreed, adding "Provided it isn't tame and goody-goody. For tameness is dulness, and dulness is boredom, and boredom is the happy hunting-ground of the Devil!"

> "Try your hand at 'Harold,'" he wrote to me later, apropos of the Sagas, "but don't try to make him cover more than just Edward the Confessor up to Battle of Hastings.
> "My idea is (I) Boadicea. (2) The Coming of the English. (3) The Coming of the Christians. (4) King Arthur. (5) King Alfred and the Danes. (6) Canute. (7) Harold.
> "The disadvantage of Harold is that you have Lytton at once to contrast and to imitate. "However try. Make the culminating scene be where Edith the Swan-Neck recognizes Harold. ... Remember as dramatic as possible, and as vivid and coloured, and no twaddle or moralizing."

He scattered his ideas in handfuls, like a sower sowing seed, and to be of any use to him one had to grasp the flying seeds of inspiration, and work them up in one's own way.

Another of his favourite journalistic maxims was—

> "Be brief. Write as though you had to cable your copy at a pound a word!"

Yet another frequent admonition to the literary aspirant was to—

> "Fall in love with somebody, preferably a woman old enough to be your mother, with whom you can only communicate to writing and are so much in love that you cannot help writing in her every day. If that does not make you write your best, nothing ever will!" And "It needs a squeeze of lemon," he said of an article excellent but dull. "It does not grip."

4

Who Is Julia?

I T WAS IN THE EARLY nineties that Mr. Stead's interest in matters psychic began rapidly to develop. The two most potent factors in this connection were, of course, his personal discoveries in automatic writing, and the passing-onward and return of Julia Ames. But its very first outward manifestation was the publication in 1891—as the Christmas Number of the *Review of Reviews—of Real Ghost Stories*, that compact little vade mecum of testimony to the truth of certain supernormal occurrences, the evidence for which was sent to him in most cases at first hand by persons who vouched for the good faith of their narrations.

This very practical attempt to "rationalize the consideration of the science of ghosts" covered a fairly extensive field, as a glance at the "Contents" page of the volume shows. Mr. Stead remarked in his Introduction—

"There seems to be a growing interest in all the occult phenomena to which this work is devoted. It is in evidence on every hand. The topic is in the air and will be discussed and is being discussed whether we take notice of it or not."

He therefore gave his readers ample food for discussion in such chapters as "The Vision of the Out of Sight," Premonition, or Second Sight,"—in which he relates the three examples of his own faculty of pre-vision already mentioned "How Phantoms come and go," "Ghosts keeping Promises," "Evil Spirits, and Phantoms which touch," "Dreams and Dreamers," and many another example of "the reality of the 'Invisibles,'" a reality which, he declared years afterwards, had long ceased to be for him a matter of speculation.

That such incursions into the psychic realm were not desirable for everyone, he readily agreed, and at the suggestion of "Catholics, Theosophists, and Spiritualists" he printed at the beginning of the volume the following "Caution" to the reader—

"PLEASE NOTE—

"I. That the narratives printed in these pages had better not be read by any one of tender years, of morbid excitability, or of excessively nervous temperament.

"2. That the latest students of the subject concur in the solemn warning addressed in the Sacred Writings to those who have dealings with familiar spirits, or who expose themselves to the horrible consequences of possession.

"3. That as the latent possibilities of our complex personality are so imperfectly understood, all experimenting in hypnotism, spiritualism, etc., excepting in the most careful and reverent spirit by the most level-headed persons, had much better be avoided."

It need hardly be said that this novel incursion of journalism into a region hitherto more or less appropriated by mystics and the Psychical Research Society, aroused widespread interest.

There has been continuous testimony to the consolation given to the bereaved by *Julia's Letters from the Borderland*, which Mr. Stead published long afterwards; but it is a less well-known fact that numbers of persons, once agnostic, were led to make their first inquiries into the reality of a spiritual world by the possibilities first suggested to them not so much by those "Ghost Stories" themselves as by Mr. Stead's practical open-minded consideration of various phenomena and happenings which had formerly been contemptuously disregarded as the result of superstition and imagination, while, farther back still, those who claimed any first-hand knowledge of such phenomena frequently suffered death by fire or water as the reward of having been born some centuries "before their time."

The appearance of *Real Ghost Stories* was succeeded the following year by *More Ghost Stories*. Both these Christmas numbers were re-published later, in one volume, by Messrs. Grant Richards, and yet another edition was issued by Mr. Stead in 1905. It is interesting to note that in his "Parting Word," at the end of the companion volume to *Real Ghost Stories* he hails with pleasure and hopeful satisfaction "the initiative so boldly taken by Professor Oliver Lodge" at a previous meeting of the British Association, and hopes that "it may be resolutely and persistently followed up." One can well imagine Mr. Stead's renewed interest when, long years afterwards, in September, 1913, Sir Oliver, speaking again to the British Association, from the Presidential Chair, once more boldly takes the initiative and affirms that his own investigations during the intervening years have convinced him that "memory and affection are not limited to that association with matter by which alone they can manifest themselves here and now, and that *personality persists beyond bodily death*." One can also picture our Chief's bluff after-comment, uttered with his own inimitable smile —

"Well, I guess it has taken Sir Oliver a jolly long time to find that out!"

From 1891 onward Mr. Stead continued ardently to pursue his own explorations in the fascinating new ground that had opened out before him as a land of infinite promise. In 1892 he made the discovery that he possessed the gift of receiving communications in automatic writing through his own hand. In that year he again published a psychic Christmas number, entitled *From the Old World to the New*, which aroused much attention, especially in esoteric quarters, for he stated in the preface that certain mysterious occurrences narrated in the story were founded upon fact.

Briefly, to recapitulate an oft-told tale, as he told It to me, his automatic-writing experiences came about in the following manner. He learnt from a lady then in his office (the daughter of an officer in the Indian Army) that she possessed the power of receiving communications in automatic writing, that is, her hand sometimes wrote apparently "by itself "and made statements concerning matters of which she herself knew nothing, but which she had subsequently found to be true. Mr. Stead was rather more sceptical than convinced that the agency was a spiritual one, and still more sceptical was he when further messages were given, stating in effect that he himself could receive communications from the Other Side, in the same way. He roundly disclaimed having any powers of the kind, but at last, after much pleading from the Invisibles, he with no great alacrity allowed himself to be persuaded to try.

When one remembers that his early attempts were made sitting at a table in his favourite restaurant, it is not very surprising that it was unsuccessful! He described it all to me at luncheon once, years afterwards, in the same restaurant. The same lady, the "Miss C—" of former years, was present also. I remember the conversation afterwards turning upon the "luckiest moments of life," and Mr. Stead's declaring with conviction, "Why, the luckiest moment of my life was, of course, when Julia first wrote with my hand!"

This is how finally that "luckiest moment" arrived. After persistent implorings, through Miss C.'s hand, by one "Frederick," on behalf of a spirit calling herself Mrs. D., Mr. Stead took up a pencil and tried for a few minutes to receive the latter's message, but without result. For "five minutes more" he was prevailed upon to allow the insistent Mrs. D. to make a second attempt, but again with blank failure. He was more convinced than ever that automatic writing was not for him. Some days later, however, the discarnate lady again returned to the charge, asking urgently that he would grant her a few minutes in the morning, before he began his work for the day. He, still very incredulous, agreed, adding—

"Well, I'll do it on this one condition, that if nothing comes of it you will never ask me to do it again!"

Doubtless the Invisibles knew the issues that trembled in the balance as the result of that reluctant promise. For the third attempt, which he duly made at home the next morning, was far from a failure. Slowly and with hesitation his hand began to move and at length a message was written, from the lady calling herself Mrs. D., which, though tremulous and almost illegible, read certainly like sense and reason. Yet in spite of the writing he remained sceptical, and it was not until by degrees he obtained the most convincing proofs of identity, memory, and personality, that at last he accepted this hitherto unsuspected development of human faculties as a perfectly provable fact, namely, the power of a discarnate person, or at any rate of some discarnate persons, to communicate in writing through the hand of another person still in the physical body.

The source from which, in those early days, he obtained the most striking and valuable proofs of survival, was Miss Julia Ames, an acquaintance of his own, who had died not many months before, after a short and sudden illness. She was a native of Maine, U.S.A., a journalist by profession, being co-editor of a Chicago paper called The Women's Union Signal, and a close friend of Miss Frances Willard, who was afterwards associated with Lady Henry Somerset in writing a short Memoir of Julia, entitled *A Young Woman Journalist*.

Despite her life of practical contact with the work-a-day world, Julia seems to have had a lurking vein of sympathy with the occult, for one learns of a pact made between herself and her dearest friend that whichever of the two should be the first to leave the physical body should if possible try to appear to the other after death, from the spirit-land. But she was certainly not a spiritualist in the ordinary sense of the word, for I remember Mr. Stead's telling me that on the two occasions on which he met Julia in the earth life, though they talked of nearly every subject under the sun, they never once mentioned Spiritualism. And that is noteworthy in itself, for it is most unlikely that Mr. Stead within recent years could have had two long talks with a kindred spirit without the word "Spiritualism" being mentioned a good many times. He used to say, "Never be ashamed to call yourself a Spiritualist. Remember that the name Christian was first used as a nickname and a term of reproach."

It was while she was editing the *Women's Union Signal* that Julia had first come into touch with Stead. I have seen the first note written by her to him, just a brief, friendly missive, asking him to send one of his inspiring messages for the readers of the *Women's Union Signal*. Of the splendid work carried on by these leaders of social reform on both sides of the Atlantic Mr. Stead wrote: "It is of the happiest augury for the two branches of the English-speaking race."

Julia next came on a visit to Europe, for the purpose of seeing the Passion Play at Ober-Ammergau. It had been one of the dreams of her life, and she realized her dream in 1890. She also came to London, and saw Mr. Stead twice, once at Mowbray House—of which she wrote to an American friend, "The chief feature of my visit to London was my interview with Mr. W.T. Stead at the office of the *Review of Reviews*"— and once at Cambridge House, Wimbledon, which in those days was his home. It is a classic memory now that she had tea in the beautiful garden of Cambridge House, under the leafy branches of the old oak-tree that shades one end of the lawn, which will now go down to posterity as "Julia's Oak."

The impression left upon Mr. Stead's mind by Julia was that of a practical and sensible person, of a nature brimming over with the milk of human kindness, and filled with the divine longing to be of service to humanity. In fact of just such a personality as she has consistently proved herself to be in all her many and various communications from the other side.

The year after her return to America Julia fell ill and passed away in a hospital at Boston. Stead learnt of her death with regret; wrote of her as "a singularly beautiful character, of devoted Christian enthusiasm;" and there, for all he knew, that pleasant but brief acquaintanceship came to an end. I have re-told this story of their meeting, often though it has been told before, merely to reiterate that Julia was neither the product of Stead's "subliminal mind" nor was she a "collective hallucination," but was during her earth-life a very comely and substantial person, as her portrait shows.

One of the last to speak with Julia a week before she passed onward was Miss Lilian Whiting, author of *The World Beautiful*,—herself a close friend of Frances Willard,—who has written for me her impressions of that sweet yet strong personality, with whom her first meeting was destined also to be her last:

> "One Sunday morning in Boston during the Convention of the W.C.T.U. in December, 1891, Miss Frances Willard telephoned to me to come down in the afternoon and go with her and Lady Henry Somerset to Tremont Temple, where Lady Henry was to speak, as the crowds would be so great. I should otherwise have some trouble in getting in. I went, was taken to the platform, and introduced, for the first time, to Miss Julia Ames. We sat together on a sofa, during Lady Henry's eloquent and noble discourse. ... On the following Tuesday, the Convention having closed, Miss Willard dined with me, and I drove her down to take the train for New York. And as she was on the step she turned and said, 'Lilian, do go and see Julia Ames. She is in the New England Hospital, ill.'
>
> "She had only time to say the words as she was stepping on to the train.
>
> "I went to the Hospital. The matron said that, while Miss Ames was not seriously ill at all, they would rather she did not see any one that day. So I left some flowers and went away. Returning two days later, I learnt that Miss Ames had sat up all day and had a most lovely and beautiful day with her friend, Miss E., but the matron still thought that she had better then having talked so much not see any one else that day, but surely if I returned a day or two later I should see her. So I left messages and again came away. ... Next day I was called up by telephone to hear the message, 'Miss Ames is dead!' "She had died suddenly in the night. Her body was to be carried to the house of Dr. D—— H——. Would I go up there? I did. It was the morning. I was met by her friend, Miss E., and we sat together for a long while, in a niche of the staircase in a soft, shaded light, and she told me of the

wonderful day's communion that she and Julia had enjoyed but a few hours before.

"'Had we known it was to be our last day together,' said Miss E., 'we could not have passed it in a more deeply sympathetic communion than we did.'

"The day itself was one of those brilliant mid-December days of golden sunshine that Boston often enjoys, a day when the air is all crystal-clear, all rose and gold.

"While Miss E. was telling me those touching and impressive experiences, the casket containing Julia's body was brought in and placed in the drawing-room. She came in silent majesty, in all the royalty of her ascended life. ... Later I was taken into the room, and I bent over the still form, in all its ineffable peace and loveliness. And this—this—was how I looked, for only the second time, on the outward form of Julia Ames, from which she had so suddenly and so swiftly withdrawn that we felt it not death but translation. (*sic*)

"A day later, on a Sunday morning, precisely one week from the day on which Miss Willard introduced me to her, with the expression of hope and expectation that our meeting would initiate between us a lifelong friendship (as I feel it has) exactly one week from that afternoon, made memorable by Lady Henry's impassioned eloquence I again looked upon the outer semblance of Julia Ames, over whose still form a beautiful little service was held before taking the casket to her home in Chicago. And that is practically all."

So ends Miss Whiting's cameo-like picture of one whose passing was but the prelude to a life of transcendent service, a ministry which sought to bring into conscious touch those loved and loving ones separated by that Bridge of Sighs we call Death, but which leads to the gate of a Life to whose boundless possibilities what mortal dare set the limit?

5

His "Confession of Faith"

~

AFEW MONTHS AFTER THOSE early experiments in automatic writing he made his first public confession of faith. This took the form of an address on Spiritualism, which he delivered at the invitation of the Members of the London Spiritualist Alliance, at their old rooms in Duke Street, Adelphi. It was on the evening of March 14, 1893, and the gathering was a memorable one not only because Mr. Stead made the first speech ever delivered by him on Spiritualism, and his first appeal for the founding of Julia's Bureau, but also because he related for the first time in public the full details of his own discoveries and early experiences in the intercommunion of the two worlds. He described, moreover, some of the curious subsequent developments incidental to his experiments. I shall therefore quote the greater part of his speech;[12] for it contains much that is the foundation of what came afterwards, and which is much better told in his own words. Addressing a crowded audience, over which the late E. Dawson Rogers, Editor of *Light*, presided, Stead began by describing his first attempts to receive messages in automatic writing. He then proceeded to relate the circumstances by which he was brought into touch with Julia Ames after her passing-on.

---

[12] From *Light*, 25th March, 1893. Mr. E. W. Wallis, editor, when last I saw him less than a month before his death in Jan., 1913, kindly gave me permission to quote the speech in full.

He said—

"I was staying down at a country house on one occasion when a lady who was there asked me if I knew where she could find a medium. I asked why? She said, 'Because my most intimate friend died six months ago and we both promised each other that whoever died first should appear to the other. ... My friend has been back twice since she died. Once, about a month after she died, she came and stood by my bedside and woke me up. I was instantly wide awake, and I saw her as plainly as when she was alive. But I could not hear anything she said and she faded away. I thought it might have been an hallucination, and I did not like to say much about it, but two nights ago she came again.

I saw her perfectly distinctly. I cannot bear to think that my poor friend has come back to me twice and I cannot hear what she has to say. Do you know any clairvoyant who might be able to tell me what she wants to say?' I said, 'Yes, and when you come to London I will introduce you. In the meantime my hand is beginning to write, and if your friend is about the place she may use my hand.'

"The next morning before breakfast I tried, and immediately she wrote. She wrote her name, she wrote messages to her friend, and she gave the tests which I have given in substance in the Christmas number of the *Review of Reviews*.[13] I do not wish to go into that because it is more or less in the knowledge of most of you. ... I was very much impressed by it because my hand had written things that I knew nothing at all about, and nothing at least which had temporarily passed from the knowledge of my friend, to whom it was communicated. That item was only brought back to her memory by additional particulars being given which recalled the circumstances which had for the moment been forgotten. I came back to London, and one day I got a letter from my friend, 'do not understand this about Julia at all'— Julia was the name of her friend on the other side— 'she said she was always with me, and directing me, and here I am in great trouble and she has not given me any directions at all, and I do not believe there is anything in it.' "On the following day I put the letter upon my desk and sat down and said to Julia, 'You see what your friend says. I will lend you my hand for half an hour, and you had better write her a letter, just as though you were on this side.' I had a sheet of foolscap before me, and to my immense astonishment my hand began, 'My darling' (using a

---

[13] From the Old World to the New.

pet name with which I was not familiar). "How can you say I do not care for you when I am always with you and looking after you?' and so on. She went on to say, 'think I cannot do better than tell you what has happened to me since I came over on this side. ...' This letter was remarkable, because it gave five or six names of persons whom I did not know had ever existed. The whole thing was very startling and puzzled me. I did not quite like it. I thought it was rather too much to profess to have a letter written in terms of the greatest endearment to a person still living. I thought I had better keep that letter over until I could find out surreptitiously whether any of those persons ever existed who were named in it, because it was playing doubles or quits to send that letter.

"The next day I put my hand upon the paper my hand never writes without permission—I have got a detachable hand, but it never gets detached unless I give it leave and said: 'Have you anything to say, Julia?' She said, 'Why haven't you sent my letter to——?' 'Well,' I said, 'you haven't finished it.' Which was quite true, although that was not my real reason. 'Never you mind that, I will finish it another time. Send my letter to her.' It was quite evident that she was not going to write anything more until I had sent the letter to Miss——; so I sent it, and waited with fear and trembling to see what the result would be.

"Two days passed and then Miss came to my office and sat down looking very much astonished. 'Oh, Mr. Stead,' she said, 'there is no doubt it is Julia; you did not know any of those people.' That took a weight off my heart. I asked: 'Were those names right then, after all?' 'Oh, yes, I know them all except one, and that may have been right, but I do not know it.' I said: 'Who was the person who came into the room when she died, and when she was standing by the bedside looking at her body?' She said, 'That was the nurse, who nursed her through her last illness.' I asked, 'Who was Mrs. B. whom she went to see?' 'That was a widow who was her most intimate friend after myself and another.' 'And those others whom she went to see?' 'One was her little sister who died when she was three years old, another was her sister who is still living, another is her brother-in-law. The other I do not know.'

"Then I began to think that this must have been Julia, and from that time for nearly four months Julia continually wrote letters to her friend, beginning and ending just in the same way as she always had written before she died: 'My darling' and advising her about her affairs and her health, and giving her information of what she was doing on the other side, exactly as though you or I were permitted to sojourn on the other side and had come back and had written a letter with your own hand. Practically for three months she wrote a letter every Sunday to Miss——, of greater or less length. That being so, I naturally got to feel that there was no doubt whatever as to the reality and the character of the Intelligence that was moving my hand, and there were many little corroborative incidents and things which proved, I think, beyond any doubt that, whoever that Intelligence was, it was something that had access to information which I had not, which was personally deeply attached to persons in whom I had very slight interest, and which professed to have at least the capacity of communicating with us, quite indifferent to the ordinary limitations of Space and Time. For instance, in the middle of a long letter, she would say, 'Excuse me, I have to go to Chicago. I will be back in a minute.' In a few seconds she would resume the writing just the same as if you were writing and somebody had called you downstairs without any difficulty.

"When this correspondence had been going on for some time, she wrote with my hand, 'Why are you surprised that I can write with your hand? Anyone can write with your hand,' I said, 'What do you mean by anyone?' I always talk to her exactly as I would to you, only that she writes her answers instead of speaking. She said, 'Any one! People on earth, alive, can write with your hand.' I said, 'Do you mean living people?' She said, 'Any of your friends can write with your hand.' I said, 'Do you mean to say that if I put my hand at the disposal of any of my friends they could write to me in the same way that you do?' 'Yes. Try it.' I thought that seemed rather a large order, but I did try it, with this result. I am not going to dogmatize in the presence of persons who have been studying this subject all their lives. I think the best plan would be for me not to give any explanation, but simply tell you what happened to me. I put my hand at the disposal of friends at various degrees of distance, and I found that, although the faculty varied, some friends could write extremely well, imitating at first the style of their own hand-writing, sometimes for the first few words until they had more or less established their identity, and then going on to write exactly as they would write an ordinary letter. They would write what they were thinking about whether they wanted to see me, or where they had been.

"I must say nothing surprised me more at first than the frankness with which friends, who I knew were sensitive and shrinking, modest and retiring, who would never tell me anything about their personal circumstances or about money matters, would tell me in the frankest possible way their difficulties and troubles without any reserve whatever. Noticing this, I said to Julia on one occasion, 'This is rather a serious thing, because it seems to me as if there would be no more secrets in the world if things can go on like this!' 'Oh, no,' she said, 'you don't understand.' ... I said, 'Well, how is it that a person will tell me things with my hand that he would never tell with his tongue?' Then she gave this explanation: I do not give it as final, but only as her own explanation which was written with my hand. I did not invent it myself, for it never occurred to me. She said, 'Your real self will never communicate any intelligence whatever, either through the hand of a writing medium, or through your tongue that is if it is yourself that is speaking—except what it wishes to communicate, but your real self is very different from your physical self.' I said, 'How do you mean—my real self?' She said, 'Your real self, what you would call your Ego, sits behind both your physical senses and your mind, using either as it pleases. Your physical senses are used for communications between your real self and your fellow-men when they are within sight and hearing. But the physical senses are only a clumsy mechanical contrivance, at the best; the mind is also an instrument and a material instrument, but a much more subtle material instrument than the physical senses, and when the real self wishes to communicate with any person at a distance it uses the mind, but it will never use the mind to tell what is wanted to be kept secret, any more than it would use the tongue, because in all cases the real self is the master.' I said, 'How can you do it?' She said, 'Why cannot you understand? All minds are in contact with each other throughout the whole universe, and you can always speak and address any person's mind wherever that person may be, if you more or less know that person. If you can speak to that person if you meet him in the flesh, you can also speak to him and ask him to use your hand in whatever part of the world you may be.'

"It may be my defect as a medium, but I find a very great difference in people I do not find that I can communicate with all my friends, by any manner of means. I find that there are some who will communicate with extraordinary accuracy, so much so that out of a hundred statements there would not be more than one which would be erroneous. I find some who, though they will sign their names right, apparently in their own character, make statements that are entirely false. ... I said to Julia, 'How is it that when I ask my friend and he answers me, he knows nothing about it afterwards? If the real self does not communicate any intelligence except at its volition, how is it that I can get an answer from my friend without his knowing anything about it at all?' She said, 'When you speak to your friend through your hand he only answers with his mind, not with his physical senses. The real self does not always take the trouble when he has communicated a thing by the mind through the hand to inform the physical brain that he has done so. It is not necessary to do so. If it thought fit it might, but it might not. It does not necessarily require it.' It is practically in this way, to take an illustration. Say I have two clerks; and one I use for personal communication with the outside world, the other for writing. I tell the writing one to write a letter and the correspondence goes on through him, and I never tell the other clerk, whom I employ to see visitors, anything about it. The distinction between the physical self and the mental self is almost as distinct as that between the two clerks, one of whom writes and the other of whom speaks."

Referring to telepathy, as generally understood, Mr. Stead went on to say—

"I have never tried but on one occasion the ordinary telepathic experiment that is to say at a certain time of the day or night to fix my mind definitely upon a friend and will him or her to write a certain thing. I never tried it but once, and then I had a very curious experience indeed. I tried it with a lady in Gloucestershire. At half-past ten o'clock in the morning she was to fix her mind upon certain information which she wished to make known to me, and I was to sit at half-past ten and write what my pen chose to write. Then we were to post the letters so that they crossed each other, and compare what was willed in Gloucester with what was written in London. Well, I wrote a good deal and posted it, and the next morning got a letter from Gloucestershire from which it appeared I had only written about one out of six or seven distinct statements which she had strenuously willed me to write. Of course I thought the experiment had failed, but I got a letter again by return, saying: 'This is more wonderful than anything. You know that you have scarcely written anything that I willed you to write, but you have written nearly everything that kept bobbing into my mind without my will at all. When I was saying to myself, "I want to tell you so and so," it kept coming into my mind, "tell him so and so," and I thought "No, that is of no interest to him," or "that will only trouble him," and you have got all the things written down in London that kept coming as it were spontaneously into my mind at Gloucestershire at the time that I was willing you to write another set of things.'

That was the only experiment I tried of that kind. It makes no difference as to where the person is. I had quite a long letter yesterday morning from Edinburgh, and I have had letters from Germany; I have had them, but not verified them yet, from America. The communications from Edinburgh are every bit as clear as those from the other side of the street; distance does not make the slightest difference.

"I had a very curious experience today, which is new to me, because hitherto, with one or two exceptions, whenever my hand has written, say from Tom Jones or John Smith, describing a certain series of events, which have happened to him, I have usually assumed that it related to events of the past. But I was lunching today with a friend who had written with my hand yesterday, informing me that he wanted to see me very urgently, as he was in considerable trouble, and considerable difficulty, from which he must be extricated by the 25th of this month. I saw him and he said, 'I did want to see you, that part of the message is perfectly correctly written, but I do not know anything about that difficulty.' Suppose there is not a difficulty, then?' I said. He looked very grave and said, 'I do not know.' I said, 'Why?' He said, 'You remember that last time, that I was here?' I said, 'Yes.' 'And you know you had a long detailed statement concerning a trouble that came to me?' I said, 'Yes.' 'Well, you know I said there was no truth in it when you read it to me. Neither was there, but it happened three days afterwards; although fortunately it had not been altogether fulfilled.' The first half of it which was detailed in precise terms happened exactly, but the latter half did not happen."

This announcement of the possibility of automatic communications from persons still in the physical body created no little discussion amongst the audience. It was a startling, even an uncomfortable innovation. Julia's theory was doubtfully questioned, in the interesting discussion which followed. Mr. Stead characteristically said he had not come there to dogmatize, but merely to tell them what had happened to him. Then he resumed—

"Do not think that, although I have not protested against what has been said in praise of my 'courage,' I really accept it or believe it, because as a matter of fact I do not. I deserve no praise in the matter. You know the thing is very simple. Either the thing is true or it is not true. If it is true the brave man is the man who goes against it, the brave man is the man who goes against truth. Just think for a moment what truth means; suppose, for instance, that you recognize this truth as being truth, in the same way as you recognize the truth that fire burns; is it not evident that the safe thing in the long run, the only safe thing, is to recognize the truth? It is nonsense to say that a man deserves to be praised for being brave for this. No doubt he needs faith and imagination, because he risks some temporary trouble and worry, but in the long run, if he really believes, there is no room for courage except in denying the truth. This is what has always puzzled me. People say of such a one, 'What a brave man he is; how absolutely he believes in God.' It surely would require more 'bravery' to go against God. The real virtue is not bravery but faith. If you really believe, it is easy enough to be strong for the truth, because then you know you are really on the strongest side. It is easy enough for a man to stand by what he knows to be true if he really believes in God, for then he takes that line which is the line of the least resistance.

It may not be the line which seems to be of the least resistance, it often seems to be the line of the greatest resistance, but that is because people walk by sight, not by faith. The exercise of what you may call daring, would be by opposing truth and opposing God, and not by taking care to have them on your side. ... The chief difficulty comes from friends and relatives, whose opinions you value, and whose loving hearts it is hateful to pain; but as for the cackling of the geese in the Strand, well, you don't mind that, because they always did cackle and they always will go on cackling. After you have demonstrated this to be absolutely true, then they will turn round and cackle on the other side. But this side or that their cackling does not count.

"But now let us turn to the question of error: it may be the fault of what I call my automatic telepathic receiver, or the motor nerves of my brain. It may be their fault, but it is very difficult to construct a working hypothesis to account for them. When my boy was in Germany he could write many things quite correctly, as for instance that he was going to such and such a place and do such and such a thing, which were all quite true, and then in the middle he would give a long detailed statement about its being a wet Sunday and that he had nothing to read but a German Bible, and that he wished he had brought some books with him to read, etc. Yet as a matter of fact it was nothing of the sort. It was not a frightfully wet Sunday, they did not want anything to read, and they had not got a German Bible. Take another instance. A friend of mine who went to Matthew Arnold's grave on Christmas Day wrote to me on the Christmas afternoon stating exactly what had happened, how he had gone to Paddington Station, caught such and such a train, had a compartment to himself all the way, taken a ticket to Laleham. I said, 'That is wrong, you cannot take a ticket to Laleham.' 'I took a ticket to Laleham and got out there and went to the churchyard. There was no one in the churchyard except myself. I went to the grave and I put some white flowers upon it, and then came back by the train. I had a carriage to myself all the way home.' That was a detailed statement about which I knew nothing before it was written; my hand simply wrote that statement off. But mark how curiously the errors come in—and the errors interest me far more than the accuracies, because the accuracies are natural. It is natural for my friends to tell the truth and not natural for them to tell a falsehood. It was in the main all right. When I saw him I said, 'I did not know there was a station at Laleham.' 'No more there is,' he said, 'I went to Staines station.' 'Then why the mischief did you write and tell me that you took a ticket to Laleham?' He said, 'I did book to Laleham. I asked the booking clerk for a ticket to Laleham and he gave me a ticket to Staines, saying that was the station for Laleham.'

"Now mark the errors—he did not go to Paddington Station, he went to Waterloo; he did not put white flowers upon the grave, he put blue flowers there. Why these two curious little errors? That is the kind of thing that puzzles us and makes us feel that we have got to study the question a great deal more than we have yet done before we can form any theory as to the facts. ...

"I went once to a meeting where there was a very wonderful automatic writing medium, and I asked her control whether or not living people could communicate, and they wrote that they did not know. I said, 'Well, I can, anyhow,' and the control wrote, 'That is because you have a very loose soul.' I said, 'What do you mean?' The writing replied, 'I mean that your soul is very loosely connected with your body, and hence you are able to allow other minds to be hitched on to your hand; but persons whose souls are closely knit to the material framework are not able to be used in that way.' That is the only explanation I have ever had given me. The whole of this range of subjects requires to be attentively studied.

"I cannot see in a crystal I wish I could. I know several of my friends who are crystal gazers, and they see living friends more frequently than dead people. There is one very curious phenomenon that has lately come up in crystal-gazing to two of my friends independently of each other that is, seeing those curious composite animal forms, part human and part animal, which the Theosophists, I believe, call elementals, and for which other occultists have various explanations. ...

"And now," he went on in conclusion, "what I want to ask and what Julia is always pressing upon me is this: Can we, or can we not, establish a Bureau of Communication between the two sides? Julia was a very good, loving, tender-hearted creature when she was on the earth, and her view is and I printed it in the Christmas number[14] that while it is a very sad thing to see people on this side wailing for their dead, with whom they cannot communicate, it is a still sadder thing for those on the other side, because they also see the sadness of those who have passed over who are also trying in vain to communicate with those whom they have left behind. Can anything practical be done? I ask you to consider it. Can anything be done, can some centre be established whether it be a college of mediums or a Bureau of Communication, or whatever you like to call it, by which any person who has lost a friend, and who wishes to receive communications from that friend, may be able to send and receive a message as to the well-being or ill-being as the case may be, and as to the whereabouts, of that friend on the other side? Julia says that it can be done and ought to be done, and she wants me to try and get it done. She says she knows I am too busy to undertake it myself, and she says also what I believe to be perfectly true, that I am not a very particularly safe medium because I am apt to infuse something into my communications. I find it difficult to be absolutely passive. Surely, in the midst of all this development that we are passing through, it ought not to be impossible to find some trustworthy mediums who could be set apart and consecrated to that purpose? I do not know why it should not be done, if it can be done. What Julia says is that until it is done, and until it is brought home to the mind of every individual that they can communicate with the spirits of their departed friends, you will never really rob death of its sting nor convince most people that death is not the end of all things! I think that is a great thing to do. I have been thinking about the matter and it seems to me that it might be possible. You have got to be very careful and not rush things; that I fully admit; and there ought to be a test which would be regarded as conclusive as to the

---

[14] *From the Old World to the New.*

identity of the communicating intelligence. If two mediums without any communication with each other, gave an equally conclusive test as to the identity of the intelligence said to be communicating, then I think you might do something. I speak as a tyro, but I intend to put this thing through. I do not intend to dawdle round it. I want to know whether or not we can do it, or whether we cannot, or if not, why not? I thank you extremely for the great kindness you have shown in listening to me."

From that point, Mr. Stead's hand, having, to use his own words, started off on its automatic career, went steadily on, with the energy that characterized everything he did. That wonderful hand held ajar for him the door through whose opening he caught radiant glimpses of the life beyond.

"Conditions" as ordinarily understood seemed almost unnecessary for him. I have often known him take an "automatic message" while waiting in a railway-station; sometimes when travelling in the train; even now and again in the whirl of the office he has seized his fountain-pen and gravely conferred with the Invisibles. What is more, he often thus obtained surprisingly accurate and verifiable results, not only from discarnate spirits but from persons still in the physical body. It would perhaps astonish some readers to learn from Mr. Stead's speech to the Alliance that he found it possible at times to receive messages from spirits still inhabiting the physical body, as well as from those freed from it. But Mr. Stead had a wonderful gift in receiving such messages, and to the end of his life here he continued to be immensely interested in making such experiments. He once defined the process as a kind of mental "wireless." The results of his investigations were sometimes surprisingly right, at other times just as surprisingly wrong. He was varyingly successful also in his efforts to transmit his thoughts to others. I hope to go more fully into this in another chapter, and merely quote in passing an example of his "telepathic writing" which recurs to me now:—

Only a week or two before he sailed for America, I had an appointment with him at the office at Kingsway, one afternoon soon after three. I was unavoidably prevented from keeping the appointment up to time and I felt worried about it, for he had said he would wait for me, and two attempts I had made to telephone an explanation were unavailing, as each time I "rang up," the line was engaged. Hurrying into the office shortly before five o'clock, fully expecting to find the Chief had gone, I found him, however, still in his "Sanctum," wreathed in blue clouds of cigar-smoke, and awaiting me with the air of benevolent satisfaction he always wore when some "test" had turned out well.

"I knew you would come all right," he said, taking up a piece of paper that lay on the table in front of him.

"Listen to what you wrote with my hand a quarter of an hour ago." And he read:

"March 25. E.K.H. I am coming and will be with you by 5. Please wait."

The hands of the clock pointed exactly to three minutes to five!

Is it not possible, that in the familiar atmosphere of his "Sanctum" he was really as much in harmony, mentally, with his surroundings as a hermit in his cell? In matters psychic, it seems to be the mental condition that governs results. This again reminds me of an occasion when I was talking on the telephone from Wimbledon, discussing some work with Mr. Stead, who was speaking from Kingsway, and he startled me considerably by suggesting that I should there and then "Ask Julia," what ought to be done!

"But I am in a telephone call-office," I objected, "and I have not even a notebook with me. Had I not better go home, and ask her to write there?"

"Nonsense!" he called. "Get a telegram-form, and ask her to write now. She can say what she wants in half a dozen words. I will ask her to write with my hand as well, and see if she can tell us both. Ring up again in five minutes."[15]

With a resigned sigh I hung up the receiver, procured a form and a pencil, returned to the box, and allowed my hand to write a few words. The matter was not of any particular importance, but it concerned three other persons, who were unknown to me, and I had no idea which way Mr. Stead's own wishes went. When I rang up again "Well?" his voice called expectantly, "What does she say?" I read the sentence aloud. "Capital!" came a triumphant shout from the other end of the line. "She says the same with me. You are an unbelieving Thomas! Go home and never doubt anymore!

---

[15] Julia had more than once announced through Mr. 'sStead's hand that she could impress us both simultaneously with the same message in substance, and indeed had often succeeded in doing so.

6

The Story of "Borderland"

~

I N 1893 MR. STEAD BEGAN the publication of *Borderland*, a quarterly
review devoted to the investigation of the psychic aspect of life. In
his own words, he was "seeking the scientific verification of the life
and immortality which were brought to light nineteen hundred years
ago." He sought it then in the evidence afforded by the shadowy realm
wherein our ego "hovers like a star," that mysterious "borderland"
midway between the physical and the spiritual, in whose devious by-
paths so many wanderers have lost their way.

The title *Borderland* was suggested to him by Mr. J. J. Morse, the
present editor of the *Two Worlds*, whom Mr. Stead many years ago
designated "the Bishop of Spiritualism."

One of the principal features of this unique "quarterly "was the first
appearance of the "Letters of Julia," the automatic communications
already described as having been received through the hand of Mr.
Stead, claiming to be written under the guidance and inspiration of
Julia Ames.

These "Letters from the Borderland" drew forth a heavy fire of
hostile criticism from many quarters, as may be imagined; criticism
which Mr. Stead duly reproduced in the first number of the magazine
with the same dispassionate fidelity with which he recorded the chorus
of hearty welcome the "Letters" had met with from other, less biassed
minds. Some of these epistolary curiosities are worth quoting.

The Right Rev. the Bishop of Nottingham wrote:—

"The intelligence which uses your hand, and of which you are not conscious, is no other than the Devil."

The lady who was so closely associated with Mr. Stead in the compiling and editorship of *Borderland*, now Mrs. H. Spoer, is better known as Miss Goodrich Freer, and was still better known in those *Borderland* days under her much-discussed anonymity, "Miss X." Her remarkable experiences in crystal-gazing were recorded in the *Proceedings of the S.P.R.*, where they first attracted the attention of Mr. Stead. Mrs. Spoer has been kind enough to write a brief resume of the four years during which *Borderland* ran its meteoric course. Her sketch is deeply interesting, not only because it chronicles an event which will always stand to students of psychic history as a landmark indicating the wide development of a general interest in subjects hitherto regarded as more or less esoteric, but also because it gives a most vivid pen-picture of Mr. Stead himself.

In the first number of *Borderland*, Mr. Stead expressed much pleasure in also having the sympathy and counsel of his friend Mrs. Annie Besant. Mrs. Spoer writes:

"I very gladly contribute some notes as to the origin and publication of *Borderland*. It must have been in the summer of 1891 that I first came into touch with my revered and valued friend William T. Stead. I had recently contributed to the pages of the *Proceedings of the Society for Psychical Research* a paper upon 'some Experiments in Crystal Gazing.' This, in deference to prejudices on the part of my family had been strictly anonymous, and indeed the greater part of it was written not at home, but when upon a visit to Mrs. Frederic Myers, the mother of Mr. F. W. H. Myers, though it was the result of prolonged study at the British Museum, and elsewhere.

"I received a letter from Mr. Myers asking permission to reveal my identity to the well-known journalist, who had not been altogether in sympathy with the work of the Society, but who desired nevertheless to make my acquaintance. Mr. Myers added that Mr. Stead was engaged upon the work afterwards published as Real Ghost Stories, and was therefore in communication with a great number of people who might be of use to Psychical Research, and whom Mr. Myers suggested I might be the means of 'bringing into line.'

"I wrote to Mr. Stead that I hoped to call upon him when we returned to London in the Autumn, and on October 10th I paid a visit to Mowbray House, Norfolk Street, which is memorable to me in many ways. It was an adventure for a girl brought up by an elderly relative with early Victorian standards, to find herself in the presence of a non-conformist journalist, in a London office; an adventure undertaken secretly so far as my home was concerned, though with the knowledge of the friends whom I was visiting, and who had sent with me a trusted family servant.

"How well I remember the sharp scrutiny of those searching blue eyes! the most 'speaking' eyes I have ever met; and then the long bewildering two hours' talk bewildering on account of the variety, the intensity, of the vistas which it opened. 'I'm bound to get behind these psychic mysteries,' Mr. Stead insisted, using 'bound' in its north-country sense of 'destined.' 'Yes, it's difficult; all true work is difficult; I've done many a thing which was like walking upon the edge of a sword above a burning hell of enmity, and wrath, and misunderstanding. But it doesn't matter when it's got to be done. This Psychical Society of yours is one of the things down there, and it's one of the hindrances. It isn't human, it's too respectable. It is like a man that's got to be found drunk in a ditch before anything can be done with him. It's altogether too immaculate.'

"He wished me to collaborate in the book he was writing, and to lunch with him at Gatti's in the Strand one day a week, to discuss progress. I was obliged to decline, but offered to contribute anonymously to the book, in which, as a matter of fact, there was eventually a good deal of my work. 'But why not lunch, all the same?' he insisted. I was much embarrassed, and murmured that I should not be allowed to lunch in so public a place. 'But why not? the cooking is excellent.' I tried to explain that my people would regard it as too emancipated. 'Bah!' he cried, getting up impatiently, 'you've got to emancipate that girl a jolly sight more, before you'll do any good with her!'

"Within a few months changes occurred which freed me from the more extreme of the conventional austerities he so much deprecated, although, when in the following spring I agreed to become joint editor of an Occult Journal, it was still necessary that I should be known only as 'Miss X,' and that arrangements should be made which should obviate the necessity for my frequenting Mowbray House, and taking my place as a member of the staff. Rooms were taken in Pall Mall

East, and a married lady engaged as my secretary. I was to visit the office occasionally only, and to see no one except by appointment. Nothing could have been kinder or more generous than the spirit in which Mr. Stead met this necessity of circumstance, a kindness all the more generous in that he was wholly out of sympathy with the social restrictions in question. In a certain sense they annoyed him; he was specially annoyed that I declined to have my portrait published in *Borderland*. There was, however, from the journalistic point of view, a certain value in the mystery in which the personality of 'Miss X' was enshrouded.

"This however is anticipating. Occasional luncheons at a quiet restaurant were now possible, and were continued for between three and four years, the menu being always the same—filleted sole, macaroni *au gràtin*, and fruit. I lunched with Mr. Stead in September 1911, at the Holborn Restaurant, and found that, for old times' sake, he had ordered the same dishes. On that occasion he went on ordering small additions to the meal, so as to prolong the opportunity for talk while he gave me a detailed account of his relations, by means of automatic writing, with Catherine of Russia.

"Every time we met he had some plan to unfold in relation to our future publication. These plans were thought out to the smallest detail. One, I remember, was an elaborate system of preserving evidence and information upon psychic subjects letters, abstracts, newspaper-cuttings, etc. These were to be placed in envelopes of different colours. I admired its completeness, and asked if it were his own invention. 'No,' he answered, 'I learnt it where I learnt much else—in prison.' It was the first time he had alluded to this incident in his career, and not knowing the circumstances, I had felt it would be tactless to introduce the subject. Now however I was free to question him, and he dwelt upon the admirable organization of prison life, upon the kindness of his friends, especially Cardinal Manning, and other clergy, and the great advantage it had been to him to have leisure to think. 'Only one thing really disturbed me,' he said,' I had nowhere to put my hands;' turning to show me that his hands were, as usual, in his trouser pockets.

"If I agreed with him as a matter of courtesy, while awaiting conviction, he always found me out, and would almost shout at me. 'Keep your S.P.R. manners for Westminster Hall,' he would exclaim, alluding to the fact that the Society for Psychical Research held its meetings there. 'Contradict me, call me fool, swear at me if you want to, but let my soul talk to your soul—I want no phrase-making!'

"There were times when—brought up as I had been—his expressions seemed to be intolerable, even irreverent and profane, but as I came to know him better I came to realize his nearness to God, and that what seemed like undue familiarity with sacred things was only the expression of this attitude of mind.

"The production of the first number of *Borderland*, which appeared in the month of July 1893 was naturally, for me, a very anxious time. I was wholly inexperienced, and knew nothing of measuring brain products with an inch-rule, and consequently we were considerably 'overset.' This, and my many other mistakes, he endured with entire patience, and during the years of our association he never uttered one word of rebuke or reproach. After passing the final proofs, I was so utterly weary that I rushed off on a country visit, travelling northwards in a night train, to be awakened in the morning at Preston I think by a boy putting his head in at the window, with 'Morning papers, Miss? *Borderland*, Miss? newest illustrated journal?' 'Not for worlds!' I answered, to his disgust. I need not say that I bought a copy eagerly at the next station!

"The venture was most cordially received, and the newspapers said many kind things, to my great relief, for I was haunted by the fear that my ignorance and inexperience had ruined everything.

"At last, just as I had returned to town, there fell into my hands one of the monthly reviews with an article of the most condemnatory kind, especially of the contributions written by Mr. Stead himself. The criticism was so utterly destructive that I felt it ought to be answered at once, and in great distress I telegraphed to my Chief, asking for an immediate appointment.

When I reached Mowbray House the review in question lay on the window-seat of his 'sanctum' where, as usual, he was sitting with one leg curled under him, all the space within reach of his hand a foot deep in letters and newspaper-cuttings. His mind, as usual, was running upon some subject remote from the object of my visit, but as soon as possible I poured out my woes and disappointment. He was a good listener, when he once began, and heard me to the end without interruption.

"'The attack is not wholly unjust,' I concluded, 'it is that which makes it so important to answer it at once, and to say that those are some of them points we had already foreseen, and meant to deal with. The mystery is, who on earth can have written it?' 'Well, first of all,' he answered, 'we will not answer it except by mending our ways, and as to who wrote it? I did.' "'You see,' he continued, when I began to recover, 'we were going on far too smoothly; people would have forgotten us before the next number comes out. I gave them long enough to attack us, and the stupid asses let all the chances go by them, so I felt it was my job. What's more there was no one else who could do it so well. I knew all the weak points, especially my own. There's nothing pleases me better, once in a way, than getting on my hind legs and laughing at that fellow Stead! The other folks never know the worst of him; I do!' "There was a time, I think during the third year of the existence of the Review, when owing to Mr. Stead's absence abroad I was left to bring out a number entirely upon my own responsibility, except for the help and ever-ready kindness of Mr. Stead's business manager, Mr. Stout. I remember how proud we both were at producing an extra-large edition at a very much reduced cost, largely by making use of matter which had been standing in type for some time, for Mr. Stead carried his aphorism 'don't spoil a ship for a ha'porth of tar,' to extreme limits. It was the last number of the year, and my Chief signified his appreciation by sending me for a Christmas present, a deed of gift of all property in *Borderland*, to take effect in the year 1900, 'by which time,' he was kind enough to add, my commercial education would be as complete as my literary experience. I showed the document to the late Marquis of Bute, whose interest in psychical research is well known, and he congratulated me heartily, proposing himself as a partner, and saying, 'It shall be the biggest thing of the kind in Europe.' *Borderland* however did not live to 1900, and the Marquis passed away during that year.

"During this same absence Mr. Stead asked me to take charge of certain of his private benefactions and to see to their administration. It was a further revelation of his wonderful charity and large-heartedness. They were a curious collection of people, these recipients of his bounty, and after careful study of the papers connected with their stories and antecedents, and some observation of the people themselves, I could not but feel that in some cases he was being badly imposed upon. He was deeply hurt when I suggested to him, on his return, that the liberal sums expended should be administered by the Charity Organization Society.

"There were many matters upon which we could never agree, social, political, and religious; and upon these we had many a friendly discussion, but, strange as it may seem, upon none did we differ more than in regard to just those problems among which we had to work together. Mr. Stead was as definitely a spiritualist as I was definitely an anti-spiritualist. He believed in everybody until they were found out, and often afterwards, and he would seek to introduce into *Borderland* the lucubrations of people at whom 'as a disciple of Lavater I shuddered!' It often ended in the confession that these manuscripts were already paid for, followed by the regretful permission to put them into the fire! showing the same generosity of soul toward my sentiments, as toward the pockets of his innumerable proteges. He knew that I wished to agree with him whenever I could honestly do so, and in all our differences he showed unfailing tolerance and consideration. He never modified or changed a single word I ever wrote without asking my permission to do so, and on these occasions which were rare it was nearly always for some personal reason; a writer must be reviewed favourably, 'for the sake of holy poverty,' as he was fond of saying; or an argument must be pursued on some special lines, because it would 'do good' to some special group of readers."

Towards the close of 1896 "Miss X" fell out of health and was for some months absent from London, partly abroad. On her return to London she found herself still unequal to the excessive strain of co-editorial work. Mr. Stead was deeply immersed in politics; particularly was he anxious in regard to England's policy in South Africa, in which he discerned the "cloud no bigger than a man's hand." For various reasons it seemed to him that the "signposts "without which he carried on no course of action, were all pointing towards his discontinuing *Borderland* for a time, though only for a time, he fondly assured himself. In October 1897 the last number made its appearance.[16]

---

[16] "The last time I saw him," adds Mrs. Spoer, "he talked much of our work together, and greatly regretted what, even then, he called 'its interruption.' He dwelt much upon the subject of death, and the revelations which he believed that death would bring. We spoke of his son, and of others, who had passed over since we last met, and he talked more than cheerfully I may even say gaily of separation and change. He quoted some words of Penn the Quaker, 'They who love beyond the world cannot be separated by it.' Looking back, it seems almost as if he had foreseen that we should not meet again. I was returning with my husband to the East. After we had parted in Oxford Street, he ran after me and asked me to drive with him to Victoria Station that we might talk a little longer. We talked little, but were delayed on the Embankment by the descent of an aeroplane. Something in the conversation which arose out of this led me to quote a few lines from Browning which he asked me to write

Writing at the time to Professor, now Sir William, Barrett, Mr. Stead said: "20 October, 1897.

"I am awfully sorry that the last number of *Borderland* has gone to press without my having had time to notice your admirable Monograph on the Divining-Rod. I have been over in the United States, and there I heard the Secretary of the Treasury, Mr. Lyman T. Gage, speak with great admiration of the immense pains and patience which you had displayed in getting it up.

I am stopping *Borderland*, but I am going on with Julia. I hope to recommence *Borderland* in a couple of years, if all goes well." Though *Borderland* did not come to life again in two years, Mr. Stead continued his own investigations the psychic realm and its problems with unabated zeal, feeling confident that this withdrawal of the outward manifestation of his ever-increasing interest in the "mystery of Being" was but the prelude to some more useful and definite form of expression. Those wondrous human faculties, half-hidden, half-revealed, were the undoubted possession of the race.

In what way, he asked himself, might they not be developed for the further realization of his ideal: "the union of all who love in the service of all who suffer?"

---

down for him, and with these lines I will conclude, for they are of bound up with my memory of a great and good man, a Christlike character, a true friend.

"I go to prove my soul;
I see my way as birds their trackless way.
I shall arrive! What time, what circuit first
I ask not; but unless God sends His hail
Or blinding fireballs, sleet or stifling snow,
In good time, His good time, I shall arrive,
He guides me and the bird. In His good time."

7

"The Signpost"

⁓

"I had always said I would never make my final pronouncement upon Spiritualism until someone near and dear in my own family passed into the Great Beyond. Then I should know whether Spiritualism stood the test of a great bereavement, bringing life and immortality to light. And I am here tonight to tell you that the reality of my son's continued existence, and of his tender care for me, have annulled the bitterness of death."

THUS, AT LAST, WAS THE signpost given for the founding of Julia's Bureau.

The cessation of *Borderland* had marked the close of another chapter in its founder's life. For a moment, so to speak, he rested on his oars and watched the flowing tide. He had made a comprehensive survey of the whole sea of psychic phenomena and had made it accessible to the general public, by acquainting them, in popular phraseology, with the results of the specialized labours of those who were painfully exploring the byways of psychology and hypnotism in search of "more light." But while, to study the enigma of life in the name of science is accounted praiseworthy, to study it in its deeper spiritual aspect of "the larger hope "and in the simple belief that "if Christ be not risen from the dead then is our preaching vain," was then, even more than it is now, considered a painful sign of credulity and eccentricity.

Mr. Stead wrote, at Christmas 1897, when publishing "Letters From Julia" in volume form, and again facing the "lions in the path":—

> "No one who knows anything of the prejudice that exists on the subject will deny that I have no personal interest to serve in taking up the exceedingly unpopular and much ridiculed position of a believer in the reality of such communications. For years I have laboured under a serious disadvantage on this account both public and private. I am well aware that the contents of this preface will be employed in order to discount or discredit everything I may do or say for years to come. That is unfortunate, no doubt, but of course it cannot be weighed in the balance compared with the importance of testifying to what I believe to be the truth about these messages written with my hand."

It has since fallen to my lot to read most of the letters which came to Mr. Stead, to the end of his life, from all parts of the world, in grateful appreciation of Julia's ministry of love and service. Part of my work for him involved the personal answering of a great number of these missives, and as in most cases this again led to a continuous correspondence with the writers, it will readily be seen how the name of "Julia" seemed to be a kind of central star whose rays extended far and wide, into China, Australia, New Zealand, Hindostan, into Africa from the Cape to Cairo, even to the remote islands of the Southern Sea.

Ten years had followed the cessation of Borderland and the publication of the first edition of *After Death*, in 1897, before the event occurred which, more than anything else, focussed Mr. Stead's thoughts on what he loved to call "the Land of Realities," This was the death, under circumstances of peculiar pathos, of his eldest son, Willie. It is rather curious to note that the month of December contains at least two anniversaries of special moment to Mr. Stead in relation to the psychic aspect of his life; one was the death of Julia Ames on the nth of December, 1891, while Willie Stead, that most gentle of souls, passed into the realm of clearer vision on the 14th December, 1907.

During the summer months immediately preceding his transition, I had occasion to have several interviews with Mr. Willie Stead during his father's long-continued absence at the Peace Conference at the Hague, and I was indebted to him for some kind and practical counsel in literary matters. Just as vividly in my memory as the day I had first seen him with his father at Newcastle, nearly sixteen years before, stands out in clear relief the last time I ever saw him on earth, at Mowbray House, in

October 1907, just after his father's return from the continent. Mowbray House seemed suddenly to have lost the atmosphere of tranquil routine into which it had fallen during the absence of its Chief, and had assumed the condition of a hive of bees at swarming time. A stream of callers was passing to and from the "Sanctum," and I, knowing my business could wait, decided not to encroach further on the winged moments of "going-to-press day." Just as I was leaving the office, however, Mr. Willie Stead crossed from his room, and on seeing me, came forward with his usual sunny smile.

"But you are not going without seeing my father, are you?" he asked.

"I shall come tomorrow," I said.

"I have sat here counting the strangers passing in and out.

His friends must wait."

"No, that won't do at all. Stay and see him; he is expecting you. Do not go yet, unless you must." Just as he spoke the door of the "Sanctum" suddenly opened and a solemn-looking individual was, as it were, shot outside, Mr. Stead's voice calling a jovial valediction after his "parting guest":—

"Well, goodbye, goodbye, my dear sir. Don't talk of peace, peace, when there is no peace. If we don't get to press today there won't be much peace for anyone in this office!"

With an amused and affectionate glance in the direction of his father "Willie" shook hands with me and disappeared into his own room. I never saw him again. Next moment I found myself in the "Sanctum," Mr. Stead telling me that he had been round half the world since he saw me last, and would probably be going round the other half before he saw me again!

This announcement referred to the "Peace Pilgrimage" of which even then he was dreaming, planning to start in the early months of the following year, making his son editor-in-chief of the *Review of Reviews*. His idea was that a dozen members of the Hague Conference should undertake a six months tour round the world, explaining in every capital the work already done by the Conference, and the problems that lay ahead. But that was not to be. Six weeks later "Willie" was called hence, and the Chief had to shoulder his burden without the earthly help of that beloved "right hand." For the time his dream of the Pilgrimage was abandoned.

One wonders whether but for Willie's death the Bureau would have ever come into being. His own sorrow brought home to Mr. Stead more acutely than ever humanity's most poignant need. What had been an eager interest in the immense potentialities of the ego, a search for an ever-surer answer to the age-long question, "If a man die, shall he live again?" became now a longing to share with all who mourned the loss of their loved ones the "glad tidings" that had come to him. "Willie has gone to work for me on the other side," he said to me a week or two after. "He was so good so kind he had nothing more to learn here. He will soon let me know what he is doing for me there, and what more I have to do in the time that is left to me now. ..."

But despite his brave smile I remember how his voice faltered at the last words, and how he suddenly thrust his hand across the mist that dimmed his eyes.

At the time of his death, Mr. Willie Stead was engaged in some historical sketches, dealing principally with Old London, in collaboration with Miss Dora Greenwell McChesney, a god-daughter of the American poetess, Dora Greenwell, and herself a writer of skill and promise. A strange fatality has attached itself to this work. After Willie's death Mr. Stead asked me to undertake his son's unfinished chapters, intending, himself, to write an Introduction to the book, which was to be published in connexion with the then forthcoming Pageant of London, in the spring of 1908. But the pageant was twice postponed, the second time in consequence of the death of His Majesty King Edward, and when finally it took place it was as part of the Festival of Empire at the Crystal Palace. The scheme of arrangement was entirely altered from what had been the original programme, thus rendering it impossible to publish our book in connexion with the Pageant. Mr. Stead therefore decided to issue the book on its own merits, in 1912, as a series of historical sketches. But before this could be done the *Titanic* had .sunk in mid-ocean, and scarcely a month afterwards Miss McChesney also had passed into the Beyond, leaving the work, still unfinished, in my hands.

8

"The M.P. for Russia"

~

A S ALL KNOW WHO HAVE experienced it, one of the great
pleasures of working for Mr. Stead lay in the knowledge of
his exceeding consideration and patient understanding of all
difficulties. The infinite variety of one's occupation, also, was in itself
a charm. In the month of January 1908 he suddenly switched me off
the "London book" to do some special secretarial work for him—which
he said "needed the wand of some good fairy"—in connexion with a
book he had had on hand for a long time but had suddenly made up
his mind to finish. This consisted of the "Reminiscences" of Madame
Olga Novikoff, the friend and confidante of statesmen and diplomats,
god-daughter of the Tsar Nicholas II, and "unofficial representative"
of Russia in England, whose ardent and pacific work towards a closer
rapprochement between these two nations when both were on the brink
of war in the stormy seventies, had caused Lord Beaconsfield to name
her "the M.P. for Russia."

The work in this connexion was of an exceptionally interesting nature,
for Mr. Stead turned over to me almost the whole of the correspondence
requiring to be dealt with in relation to the book. That is, the letters
received by Madame Novikoff from the many persons of international
fame, social, political, artistic and literary, who formed her *salon* in the
latter part of the nineteenth century; also much of the contents of Mr.
Stead's own pigeon-holes, covering the same period of time. These I was

to read and put in order ready to his hand. Many were to be copied, and a certain number were to be translated from the French. They embraced a great variety of themes, and the task of arranging them promised to be a fascinating one, though at first sight it looked decidedly formidable, and I remember quaking inwardly as I drove off in a four-wheeler with the first huge batch of material, the Chief's parting benediction ringing in my ears: "Just scramble through them and come and see me on Tuesday with the questions you will need to ask." It was at any rate a relief to feel he realized I might need to ask some questions!

On arriving home with my precious freight I began at once to unfasten and examine package after package of the letters of such eminent personages as Gladstone, Froude, Kinglake ("Eothen"), Edward A. Freeman, Professor Tyndall, Emile de Laveleye, and many another of the famous men and women who had done homage to Madame Novikoff in bygone days. Mr. Stead was very anxious to have them as soon as possible; and for my part I was no less anxious to show him that the "wand of the good fairy" had been at work.

I had been engaged upon them for some hours when a telegram was put into my hand. I opened it, supposing it to be some further instructions from Mr. Stead. It was not from him, however, but was to inform me of the sudden death, that morning, of a near and dear relative, in the north of England, and to desire my presence with her family next day.

In addition to the great shock of such unexpected news was the distress and embarrassment of having to put aside work of such moment, which had only just been entrusted to me. Early next morning I called at Mowbray House and saw Mr. Stead, explaining to him what had happened.

How inexpressibly kind and sympathetic he was; and how urgently he bade me dismiss for the time all thought of the letters from my mind, and to stay in the north as long as I should be needed. The January number of the *Review of Reviews* was just out, I remember, and he put a copy into my hands as I left him, saying simply, "I have written about Willie." It contained his character-sketch of his son just four weeks after the latter's death and I read it in the train on my long, cold journey northward, with newer understanding of all it meant to him. Next morning, in the house of sorrow, the early post brought me a letter from Mr. Stead and a copy of *After Death*—the first I ever had. It lies before me now as I write, with its inscription, dated January 1908, written with his own hand on the "Rosary "page—

"TO MY GOOD FAIRY, From W.T. STEAD."

With his keen, intuitive sympathy he had divined my anxiety lest he should be unable to await my return to my interrupted work, and he sought to allay it by the graceful words I have just quoted in his gift of "Julia's Letters." By such constant expressions of his wonderful and unfailing lovingkindness he endeared himself to us all. It has been well said of him that he had a "genius for friendship." He had, too, the exquisite faculty, or instinct, of knowing exactly what to say, for he lived in "the supreme moment," not in spasms, but always.

One of the most beautiful ideas expressed by Julia through the hand and mind of Mr. Stead was what she called the "modernizing of the Rosary." As everyone knows who has read *After Death* there are a number of blank pages bound up at the end of the book on which the reader may write the names of the various persons and causes which stand in different relations to his life. Those names represent the beads of the rosary. Julia's idea was that this list of names should be scanned every morning, or, if time would not then allow, at any other spare moment during the day, and a loving thought sent out to each at the moment of reading.

This modernizing of the Rosary, wrote Mr Stead in recording Julia's suggestion, would help to send an enormous stream of those loving thoughts which are as the divine life-blood of humanity, pulsing throughout our daily lives; and to all Companions of the Rosary he commended Julia's words, that a thought of love is as "an Angel of God, sent to carry a benediction to the soul."

9

Automatic Writing

~

I
T WAS ABOUT THIS TIME that I began to make further experiments
for myself in automatic writing, a subject in which, some years
before, I had taken a certain amount of interest. The writing, after
the usual preliminary scrawls, came fluently enough, but I could not
feel by any means always sure as to the identity of the intelligences
which purported to be using my hand. Mr. Stead, however, was perfectly
satisfied that some of these messages came from his son Willie. The
latter communications were invariably addressed to Mr. Stead and
occasionally contained information which I had no normal means
of knowing, besides being, as he said, absolutely characteristic of his
son's thought and mode of expression. This, together with the intense
pleasure it gave him to receive these messages, and his eager desire
that I should continue to transmit them, made me, from time to time,
readily place my hand at the disposal of my invisible friends.

It was not till a year after Willie's passing-on that he began to
write through his father's own hand. During the first few months of
bereavement Mr. Stead shrank from allowing him to do so, fearing
lest his own anxiety might tend to obscure the communications. But
on New Year's Eve, 1908, in the study at Smith Square, Westminster,
in the presence of his sister Estelle, Miss Scatcherd, my mother and
myself, Willie wrote his first message through his father's hand, over
which there was great rejoicing.

When Mr. Stead was in Russia during 1908, he was most urgent that I should allow "Willie" to continue to write for him while he was abroad. One day I received a communication signed "W.S., Junr.," expressing a certain amount of anxiety, and stating that his father was "up against the Holy Synod." In some trepidation, for the message had no significance to my mind, I sent it on to Mr. Stead in St Petersburg. He replied at once confirming the purport of the message, which evidently related to an effort he was then making to obtain permission for the Salvation Army to enter Russia, a prospect not unnaturally disquieting to the heads of Greek Orthodoxy. He had just discussed the matter with M. Stolypin, the Prime Minister of Russia and Minister of the Interior.

He wrote the same week:

"I have had a nice message from Julia. ... She says that in what is left of my life I am to know more of the Passion of the Love of God, and that my chief work lies ahead."

While on this visit to Russia—his last, as Fate had ordained—he also made a flying visit to Finland, where he had many friends and admirers. With unabated energy he returned to London early in August, just in time to run down to Cowes, to meet the *Indomitable* which was bringing the Prince of Wales (now George V) home from Canada. As an example of the journalistic *coups* in which W.T. S. revelled, the story of his meeting the *Indomitable* is characteristic and amusing. Lord Fisher afterwards recalled it thus:

"Stead is the first of Journalists. I know, because he beat me so hollow in a match in which I had all the cards. It was when the Prince of Wales returned from Canada. I took every precaution to keep the Press at bay. Stead hired a little dinghy, came up to the warship in the twilight, scrambled up the rope-ladder a daring feat for an elderly landsman got on deck, marched along with his own superb assurance, talked to officers who never dreamed that such an air could belong to an intruder, returned, tumbled down the ladder and gave his paper the only great story that appeared in the Press next day."

Mr. Stead on that occasion was acting as Special Correspondent for the *Daily Mail*. His article dated "Cowes, Monday midnight," appeared in the *Daily Mail* of August 4, 1908.

He lost no opportunity of giving full publicity to developments in psychic affairs, in the *Review of Reviews*. In February, 1908, he referred with appreciation to Sir Oliver Lodge's address at the annual meeting of the Society for Psychical Research as being among the events in the Progress of the World, of interest and importance "as showing how near we are coming to a scientific demonstration of the persistence of the personality of the Individual after the change we call death." Regarding the Society's experiments "in intelligent co-operation with the late Mr. Myers and Dr. Richard Hodgson," Mr. Stead observed that Mr. Myers himself "will find it difficult to surmount the obstacles which his exaggeration of the doctrine of a subliminal consciousness has placed in the way."

Later in the same year, 1908, he wrote a review of the automatic writing of Mrs. Holland, which had been published in the S.P.R. Proceedings for June. His article contained some deliciously candid criticism of what he called the Society's "jargon and cant."

> "It used to be said of old time that if you wanted to keep a profound secret there was no more effectual method than that of publishing it in a Blue Book. The Blue Book is, however, popular reading compared with the little Green books wherein the S.P.R. bury from sight and memory of man the records of such occasional phenomena as are forced upon their attention despite all their efforts to remain uninformed."

Regarding Sir Oliver Lodge's now famous metaphor of the working parties tunnelling from opposite sides of a mountain, Mr. Stead objected that the S.P.R. is:

> "no tunnelling working party. Its deceased members may be tunnelling through the mountain on the other side, but instead of being met half-way by their colleagues, approaching from this side, they find their chief difficulty in the obstructions, the purely artificial obstructions, which the Society has placed in their way."

But, he concluded, with characteristic humour,

> "As some of the workers from the other side were themselves responsible in their earth-life for the creation of these obstacles, it is perhaps only just that they should have their full share in removing them."

Before the appearance of this article in the *Review of Reviews*, and before I had read a word, either of it or of the messages to which it referred, he suddenly announced one day that he was perfectly certain Mr. Myers could write through my hand if I would only "give him the chance," I had read a portion of Myers' *Human Personality* some three or four years before, but knew nothing of him otherwise, except vaguely as a leader of psychical research, nor had I read any of the Verrall-Holland cross-correspondence. Therefore it was with great reluctance that I sat down, at home, that same evening and awaited the result of which my Chief was so confident. Presently my hand moved, and a long screed was poured forth. On my forwarding it to Mr. Stead he replied, "Myers' message is most interesting and most characteristic," and he thereupon appended it (under the initials E.K.H. in deference to my desire for anonymity) to his article, which duly appeared in the September issue of the *Review of Reviews.* Sir William Crookes, the present President of the Royal Society, was sufficiently interested, on reading the article, to suggest through a friend that Mr. Stead should endeavour to obtain from Mr. Myers messages on the cross-reference principle. Mr. Stead at first refused, then afterwards he thought the experiment might be worth attempting. At about that time, being far from well, he went for a few weeks' rest to Ealing, intending, while there, to complete *The M.P. for Russia*, which, he declared plaintively, "will never get done unless I am out of reach of the telephone-bell!"

During his stay at Ealing Mr. Stead wrote suggesting that I should allow my hand to write the first part of a sentence every morning at half-past nine, my mind to be a blank, my pen moving as it pleased. After half-past nine he would allow his own hand to write the second part of the sentence. We were then to exchange postcards, each card bearing the half-sentence received in the morning, also giving a record of dates and hours. I complied with pleasure, feeling that even if our experiment were a dead failure it would at least help to break the monotony of captivity for our "caged lion." Accordingly we carried out this plan for fifteen consecutive days, duly dispatching and receiving our postcards morning and evening. The result was fifteen sentences, of which eleven, so far as they went, were complete. Mr. Stead, when publishing the result of the experiment later, remarked that he did not for a moment put forward these sentences as a proof that the controlling intelligence was actually Mr. Myers, but as an indication that there was some unseen intelligence which could successfully communicate sentences in halves to two persons who received them by automatic writing though separated by a distance several miles. Once, for instance, "Mr. Myers," when writing with my hand, finished abruptly with the word "and"; then my pen, seeming to hesitate, added "or." I mentally asked whether the word "or" were merely an interpolation of my own mind. My hand at once wrote: "*And* is quite correct, but Gurney who is here this morning wished to substitute *or*. Hence your receiving cross-vibrations. This may possibly affect Stead." Mr. Stead, in referring to this, wrote: "The curious thing was that I (the same morning) also received the word "and" at the beginning of my half of the sentence, as if to emphasize his protest against what he described as Gurney's "ill-advised but entirely well-meant suggestion." The complete sentence, when both halves were fitted together, ran:

"Fellowship of mutual sympathy is the best equipment and (and) whatever happens do not flinch."

I have gone into these details because this was really the beginning of our long sequence of "automatic" communications. From that time forward, month in, month out, scarcely a day passed that my Chief and I did not exchange letters containing some script from one or other of our invisible friends. "I pray with my pen," he once said, in allusion to the beautiful, mystical reveries, musings of a higher Being, which were expressed at times through his mind and hand, in answer to his soul-searchings, his deepest questionings. These communications, before being placed in his psychic archives, usually went the round of the little group of intimate friends whom he called his "hierarchy of the innermost inner." In the archives also repose the greater number of my own "autoscripts "received during those precious and unforgettable years.

As an example of one of our "cross-reference" messages, received in two separate parts, when my Chief and I were some seventy or eighty miles apart, the following will serve. It was not one of the Ealing "cross-sentences," but came about two years later, apropos of a book he was reviewing, Sir Oliver Lodge's *Survival of Man*. On the last page of his lengthy review, which appeared as the Book of the Month in the *Review of Reviews*, December 1910, Mr. Stead wrote as follows:

"I had written up to this point when the idea occurred to me of asking one of Sir Oliver Lodge's friends on the other side to write the concluding passage of this review, using for that purpose the hands of two automatists, one of whom had read the book and the other had not. Each automatist wrote independently, at a distance of seventy miles, and the second did not know where the script of the first had broken off. The reader will find it difficult to indicate the precise point where one message ends and the other begins."

Here followed the autoscript. One part had come through Mr. Stead's hand, the other through mine. The two separate portions joined together read thus:

"'sir Oliver Lodge has conferred a signal benefit upon his generation by the courage and persistency with which, albeit in guarded and cautious language, he has affirmed the truth of the life after death. If his statements should appear to be somewhat too hypothetical and his conclusions to be put forward too tentatively, it is only in form. In substance he is now publicly committed to all the essential doctrines which have heretofore been regarded as the monopoly and the reproach of the despised spiritualists. The fact of the survival of personality after death, the demonstrated reality of holding converse between the discarnate and the incarnate, the essentially human interest and activities of the dead, and the constant and continuing influence of spirits upon mortal men, all these are affirmed by Sir Oliver Lodge in his book with no uncertain sound. Its publication marks an advance, not perhaps so sudden and decisive an advance as that of some which have taken place in the past, but nevertheless a definite advance to a position which has heretofore been left to be defended by the Uhlans who ride far in advance of the main army. The pioneers like all pioneers have had a hard time in their warfare against materialism and the still more antagonistic forces of social prejudice and so-called religious dogma. But now that Science has added the weight of her testimony, and combined her orderly array of carefully-sifted evidence with the stirring records of the free-lance fighters the blending together of the two streams of energy marks the opening of a new and epoch-making chapter in the long story of man's onward progress from the Cave to the Stars.'[17]

With regard to the handwriting, Mr. Stead wrote:

---

[17] See Appendix.

"The usual question asked by sceptics is whether the messages are in the handwriting of those from whom they purport to come. To this the answer is sometimes yes, sometimes no, but it is a matter of no importance. Those on the other side are usually content if they can control the medium sufficiently to convey their ideas without worrying to reproduce their calligraphy. But sometimes the handwriting is exactly reproduced." [18]

[18] *Review of Reviews*, November, 1908.

10

"Memories"

~

"Would Stead have purified Spiritualism, or would
Spiritualism have contributed to the aggrandisement of his
soul? What does it matter? Such as it was, his soul was one of
the most beautiful reflections of the divine upon earth."

—JEAN FINOT: *A FRENCH APPRECIATION OF W.T. STEAD.*

WHILE THE "O.K. BOOK"—AS MR. Stead called it—was in
progress I received bulky parcels of MSS. from him on an
average twice a day, and with them invariably came the
characteristic little notes of instruction and encouragement by which
he made the most tedious tasks interesting; for, as was said of Ruskin,
our Chief "never wrote a purely business letter; there was always
something personal in it, some intensely human touch." I have many
hundreds of such missives. They bring to mind his own words written
after the passing of Cardinal Manning—the memory of whose fatherly
goodness towards him he unceasingly cherished:

"When I look over the letters he sent me, now that he has gone and I
shall receive no more the notes in his familiar hand, I am filled with

wonder at the thought of all his loving-kindness, his unfailing sympathy and his invincible patience." [19,20]

It so happened that *The M.P. for Russia* was destined to be his "swan's song," the last book from his pen. "It is the story of two lives," he remarked. And so indeed it is. A story having its beginnings more than thirty years before. For in order fully to cover the ground of Madame Novikoff's immense activities on behalf of a lasting understanding between Russia and England the true keynote to the peace of Asia it was necessary that he should describe in detail much that was contemporaneous in his own life, especially in the early days, when his fierce campaign on behalf of the outraged Bulgarian Christians drew forth the admiration of the leading thinkers of the day, notably W. E. Gladstone, and Edward A. Freeman the famous historian of pre-Norman England. Gladstone frequently corresponded with the then young and unknown editor of the *Northern Echo*, recognizing the "acute discernment" with which he wrote and regarding him as his able and trusty lieutenant in the stalwart North, but it was Edward Freeman who first called Madame Novikoff's attention to his long and ardent advocacy of an Anglo-Russian *entente* and no less ardent denunciation of "Turkish misrule"; and at once she resolved to make the personal acquaintance of one who wrote of her beloved country as though he too had "Russia in his soul." It was at a time when the fire of her patriotism had been fanned into the flame of a powerful working force by the death of her brother, Colonel Nicolas Kireeff, whom she idolized. Formerly an officer in the Guards, he had volunteered in the year 1876 for active service in Servia, when the Ottoman orgy of carnage had sent the Call of the Blood ringing through the heart of the Slavonic race. Tall and of superb physique he wore a snow-white uniform, that he might be the more easily seen by his free-lances who adored him and would have followed

---

[19] Cardinal Manning's sympathy supported and sustained Mr. Stead throughout the darkest hours of the "Maiden Tribute."

[20] The Cardinal was one of the clear-seeing souls who recognized in that darkness the foreshadowing of dawn. As the Bulgarian Atrocities made W.T. 'sStead's journalistic and political fame, so the "Maiden Tribute" wrote his name in fiery letters across the world as the St. George of modern times. Soon after the loss of the *Titanic*, Archdeacon Wilberforce, speaking to me from his own remembrance of those stormy days, when no execration was vile enough to couple with the name of Stead, said: "I knew then, that he was the greatest man we had!" E.K.H.

him to the death. He fell at the head of his regiment, only twenty-five feet from the Turkish trenches, cheering and waving on his men. His body remained in the hands of the Turks, but four years later a white stone cross was placed on the spot where he fell, and a Servian village, by the wish of the inhabitants, was rebaptized by his name. Froude describes the story of Nicolas Kireeff as resembling "a legend of some mystic Roman patriot or mediaeval crusader." And Kinglake has related it with vivid detail in the Preface to his *History of the Crimean War.* Kireeffs devoted sister, no less passionately attached to his memory in death than to himself in life, from that moment made the attainment of an Alliance for Peace between Russia and England the ideal of her dreams. Mr. Stead having been for several years eagerly advocating the self-same object, it was not surprising that their common cause should become linked by a friendship which continued throughout the following years, despite many differences of opinion and alternations of political sunshine and storm.

It is a truism that history repeats itself; but in 1912, as we have seen, the curtain again was raised in the Balkans on much the same *mise-en-scene* as when, in the early seventies, W.T. Stead so eloquently pleaded the Bulgarian cause. The rally of the Slavs round Macedonia was but one more effort to throw off the hated Moslem yoke. And does not the history of the year 1914 offer a vastly magnified parallel? Austria's attack on Servia sounded the call-to-arms to which Russia again replied on behalf of her kindred, in tones so thunderous that they have shaken the Empire-kingdom of the Danube to its very foundations. The call of the Spirit is a still deeper, more piercing cry than that of Blood; and Russia, while arming on behalf of her Servian brethren, at the same moment joined hands with France and England against the dark forces of a pitiless militarism, and on behalf of yet another outraged people. The blood-sodden fields of violated Belgium have sanctified today the union of Briton and Slav.

But this digression is a far cry from the intimacies of everyday life and work. I have touched on these wider issues here only because my Chief's letters at the time he was writing The *M.P. for Russia* were full of references to those bygone events which had ploughed so deep a furrow in his life and were among the first steps of the ladder by which he was to mount to fame.

As in my memories of him I must mingle small with great, I may mention here that a favourite habit of his was to date his private letters by the name of any anniversary on which the day happened to fall. September the third, for instance, was always "Cromwell's Day" ("of double victory and death"); the day after Good Friday was "Good Saturday"; the anniversary of his son's death was "Willie's Second Birthday." Another little characteristic was his way of giving descriptive names to his friends, more or less applicable. My own activities in connection with the "O.K. Book" for I remember feeling very important and full of zeal and rather thought the heavens would fall or the sun stand still did post-time pass without "copy"—earned from him the title of "the Brownie," in allusion to the Brownie of Michael Scott which could never be supplied with sufficient work to keep it occupied. That small joke about the Brownie was kept up for some time, until it gave place to various other appellations. But it was brought back vividly to my mind some months after his death, in a manner so strongly evidential of his identity that I am tempted to relate the story here, as an example of one of those very "trifles" which Sir Oliver Lodge considers so valuable as proofs of personal memory and survival.

While staying in Cornwall during the year following the loss of the *Titanic* I chanced upon a clairvoyant, and the idea came to me to test her gifts as I was quite unknown to her. After a few preliminary remarks, of no significance, she said: "I am attracted to the locket you are wearing. May I hold it a little while?" It was a small enamelled locket, given to me soon after Mr. Stead's passing-on, by his daughter Estelle, and containing a portrait of her father, which was of course not visible from the outside. The clairvoyant held it unopened in her hand, her eyes being closed. After a few moments she said: "There is someone with you now who was drowned." I said I understood, and she added, "I have a feeling of intense cold but I cannot get any other physical condition," After another pause she began to describe a man: "rather thick-set "she called him," with grey hair and a bushy grey beard," I assented, but said nothing to connect this description with the condition of drowning she had previously felt. She next mentioned one or two small details, such as his holding up a bundle of papers, and saying something about writing. After another pause, all at once she said: "I keep hearing the word 'Brownie.' I don't know what it means, but I keep hearing it over and over again. It is not Brown, it is 'Brownie.' Can you understand?" I said I understood so well that if I never received anything more I should be quite satisfied I had been in touch with the other side. I left Cornwall the same week, without having enlightened the sensitive either as to my own identity or that of the personality she had described.

I remember a curious evidence of involuntary thought-transference which occurred between us during his stay at Ealing, as from time to time happens between persons in close sympathy. One of his letters had concluded in a somewhat downcast strain and I in reply had suggested as an antidote the 91st Psalm; with its beautiful thoughts of the ministry of angels and shadow of protecting wings.

He answered immediately:

> *"September 28.*
> "It is interesting your request about the 91st Psalm. Only yesterday I telegraphed to—— in St. Petersburg saying 'Read 91st Psalm,' as there is cholera in the street where she is staying."

Forwarding one of his autoscripts at the same time, he added:

> "I enclose you Julia's second message, on the grief of the departed 1 for those left behind, a question which comes up very poignantly. The difficulty is, as you can see, to repress questions."

Always a vast difficulty for his eager mind, ever questioning and seeking. At that time Julia was writing messages through his hand, from half-past six to seven o'clock each morning. She had expressed a great wish to write a second series of Letters, which would form a Sequel to *After Death.* She said that having now passed many years on that side she had learnt much more concerning its laws than had been clear to her at first. She would gladly teach what had been made known to her, and would answer as best she could all questions that arose during the transmission of her messages. "In this way," she said, "it will be a kind of encyclopedia of the other life which you will receive from me and the other coadjutors whom I have here. It is true that I know but little. I have been but on the seashore. But I have been there. And I will tell you what I know. ... What seems to me clear is that the simplest things are not clear. You are all more or less confused. I was myself at first. I think I can with my helpers make many things clear, so clear that it will be a great comfort to the bereaved and a great stay to the men and women who are engaged on their earthly pilgrimage and warfare."

"But," she added, "there are some things which are difficult to explain, others impossible, and some are forbidden to be explained." She began by describing the first impressions of the soul when it wakes after the change which we call death.

Her statements were afterwards confirmed by another control purporting to be F. W. H. Myers, who was asked by Mr. Stead whether his experiences and impressions confirmed those of Julia, and who wrote in reply:

> "My awakening was less a sense of bewilderment than one of intense satisfaction and peace. Then came astonishment. ... With astonishment came curiosity, the wish to explore this new world which is yet the old, and above all things an overwhelming dismay as I found wherein I had drawn so many false conclusions. The logical results—so-called—of speculative reasoning on the physical plane do not apply here at all. We have different elements and are governed by different laws."

After writing for fifteen consecutive days on various aspects of life on the other side Julia suggested that Mr. Stead should submit copies of those messages to different persons whom he knew to be interested in the subject. When he had gathered from them the various questions raised by her statements she would try to answer them in detail through his hand. When sending me the MSS, he remarked:—

> "Julia's third is rather terrible. You can understand how my mind struggled like a stormy tide, as she says. I suppose it must be true, but what a multitude of questions it raises. Write your questions on the spare page at the end of the message. I don't suppose we shall ever get through all these questions. But let us accumulate them."

Another of his unconsciously prophetic remarks. Those questions remain for the most part unanswered, though in the Spring of 1912 she had begun to answer them through his hand and to annotate through mine. Proofs of the Letters had duly been sent to a number of sympathizers, amongst them many men and women of eminence in the literary and scientific world, and the lists of questions returned opened up as may be imagined an immensity of religious, ethical, and philosophical speculation.

"Russel Wallace,[21] says that it won't come to much," remarked Mr. Stead apropos of these, "because no one can possibly describe more than a bit of the other world. Granted, but let us collect the bits!"

The month at Ealing came to an end early in October and he returned to town, writing me on the morning of his departure a regretful little

---

[21] Dr. Alfred Russel Wallace,

comment on the inevitable necessity of returning once more to the everyday whirl. The unwonted rest and comparative freedom from "rush," the daily budget of letters from his "hierarchy of friends," had been both a relief and a stimulus.

He likened it to being "by green pastures and still waters," But even during that period of supposed "rest" his day began at 6.30 a.m.—with the reading of Fenelon or a chapter from the Old Testament Prophets—and continued until 9.30 p.m., reading and writing for hours at a time. This did not in the least represent the myriad activities of his ordinary working day, into which he crowded the maximum amount of brain-work possible to be achieved by mortal. He once told me his best working hours were from 6 to 12 in the morning, and again from 6 to 12 at night. He greatly disliked to write in an afternoon, though often he did so, in order to "get through." His letters to me are sprinkled with admonitions never to work on Sunday!" We worship when we rest," he once remarked. He frequently sat up till the early hours of the morning about this time, "wrestling with proofs" and otherwise exercising the busy brain that seemed never still. Many of his letters are headed I and 2 a.m. On the other hand he had the useful faculty, at times, of being able to sleep almost at will. Throwing himself down on the sofa in his "Sanctum" he would fall instantly asleep, then in a few minutes he would wake up as suddenly and, sitting down at his table, he would take up his pen and dash into an article or letter, just where he had broken off. His ideas crystallized so rapidly, he knew beforehand so exactly what he meant to say, that he rarely needed to alter or erase; and his brain was stocked with statistics and quotations the accuracy of which he scarcely ever needed to verify. Yet if it happened once in a way that he was in doubt as to some reference he would at once cease writing and hunt through volume after volume till he had verified his point. That his memory was phenomenal is almost an axiom.

He saw the October number of the *Review of Reviews* to press, then went down to Hayling Island, from which he sent me "Julia's fifth message," with the comment:

"There is a certain grim realism about her picture of the disembodied dead beating like moths at a lighted window-pane, against the barrier that separates them from survivors.

"I am reading *John Silence*, an occult novel."

Next day, October 8, enclosing another of Julia's, he added:

> "Julia has just left me. I think she is splendid. Her serene indifference to my little ailments is good. And it is evident that she is going over the whole ground very carefully and methodically. I am allowing her to monopolize my auto-hand at present."

Again:

> "I enclose you a message from Julia. I am very grateful to her. You see she takes her own way, quite regardless of what I say. I wish I could always have this time with her in the morning. ... Is it a subtle ministering to my own vanity, a temptation of the devil to make me regard my own sins and shortcomings as essential?"

And again:

> "I have had a very remarkable message from Julia, foreshadowing a big piece of work for us all in the psychic realm."
> (A forecast of the Bureau.)

From these and similar comments it will be seen that his correspondence with the Invisibles was as real and serious a part of his life as his correspondence with his friends who were still in the physical body. To him, indeed, there was no difference. Souls incarnate and discarnate were all, "the one Army of the Living God."

11

Catherine The Great

~

T HE VIVID "RUSSIAN ATMOSPHERE" INDUCED by the writing of *The M.P. for Russia* continued throughout the autumn and winter of 1908, during which time, on his return from Ealing, Mr. Stead was still closely at work on his book. There had also been a series of unusually interesting moves on the psychic chessboard, if one may so term it, for a powerful influence, purporting to be that of no less a personage than Catherine the Second, Empress of Russia, had for some time past loomed large on our horizon, and in a variety of ways seemed endeavouring to express from the Beyond her continued interest in the future of the Slavonic peoples, of whom she frankly styled herself the "tutelary deity." Affairs in Eastern Europe were fast approaching that political and international crisis of which the principle outward feature was the annexation by Austria of Bosnia and Herzegovina.

Through several sources, including the hands of three automatic writers (Mr. Stead, Miss Scatcherd and myself) the Great Empress seemed endeavouring to convey what the Chief called a separate section or "ray" of her complex personality, the result being a marshalling of forces whose combination was, to say the least of it, imposing. She also expressed herself with great ease and fluency through Mr. A. V. Peters, the psychic, who when in deep trance often became the mouthpiece for much political wisdom concerning the affairs of Eastern Europe in general and Russia in particular.

To Mr. Stead, who did not hold the opinion that the former rulers and statesmen of the earth have "elected to pass eternity in dignified idleness" there was nothing at all impossible or far-fetched in the idea of the Imperial Catherine's condescending to utter words of counsel, guidance, and warning, in regard to the destiny of the "Holy Russia" she loved so well.

It was understood that Catherine had long been interested in W.T. Stead as an ardent worker on behalf of her adopted country, she having found in him a facile instrument through whom she could express the vast ideals left unattained by her at the close of her tumultuous reign. On this theme she constantly and variously dilated, declaring that all unconsciously to him to her unseen influence from the Beyond was due the persistent trend of his mind towards an Anglo-Russian *entente*, his persistent sympathy with the Slavonic ideal, and the constantly recurring "Russian influence" that was the dominant note of his career.

In this connection, as in others no less striking, the "long arm of coincidence"—or apparent coincidence—is evident in his life from first to last. His first employer was Russian Vice-Consul at Newcastle-on-Tyne. As editor of the *Northern Echo* ("the youngest editor in England") he first attracted the attention of Gladstone and Freeman in 1876 by his brilliant, impassioned articles on the Bulgarian Atrocities, and he was one of the "three Englishmen" to whom the thanks of the Bulgarian Assembly were publicly voted in 1878 for service rendered to the cause of Bulgarian independence. In this period began also his life-long friendship with Madame Olga Novikoff, by whom he was personally introduced to Gladstone, Froude, Thomas Carlyle, and many another of the giants who had first stirred his youthful enthusiasm. He was the first—I believe the only—journalist to "interview "a Tsar of Russia: he was received by Alexander III at Gatchina in 1888, and thrice later by Nicolas II, the present Tsar. And he numbered among his Russian friends men of such widely differing personalities as Madame Novikoff, Count Leo Tolstoy, Pobedonestzeff, M. Stolypin, and Prince Kropotkin. In one way and another he has been persistently identified with Russian affairs, and to use his own words, he has "preached, in season and out of season, an Anglo-Russian Alliance."

Apropos of the Gatchina interview with the Emperor Alexander, an amusing detail, variously told, went the round of the press at the time, concerning his "dismissing the Tsar." The true story, as the Chief told it to me, was that after a conversation lasting nearly three-quarters of an hour, Mr. Stead, feeling that he had already trespassed sufficiently long on the Emperor's time, suddenly jumped up and declared that he "really could not detain his Majesty any longer!" The Emperor's smile of mingled amusement and surprise as he also rose to his feet, "Made me feel what an ass I had been," related the Chief, adding, "If only I had gone on talking I might have had another half-hour." He had been till then all-unconscious of the "etiquette" of Courts which ordains that it is the Sovereign who brings an interview to a close. Nevertheless, it was of that famous interview with the Emperor Alexander III, that Sir Robert Morier, then British Ambassador at St. Petersburg, wrote to Queen Victoria that "never since the memorable interview between Nicolas I and Sir Hamilton Seymour had any Russian Emperor ever spoken with such frankness and fulness to any Englishman. Not only so, but the circumstances under which the interview had taken place, and the character of the interlocutors, rendered it certain that the '*verite vraie*' had been spoken."[22]

The outcome of that Russian visit of 1888 was Mr. Stead's book *The Truth about Russia*, which he published soon afterwards. That book had the curious experience of being first interdicted by the Russian Censor (in particular because of certain pages relating to religious persecution), and afterwards of having the prohibition removed, it was whispered, by the Emperor Alexander himself, after which *The Truth about Russia* was circulated freely throughout the whole Russian Empire.

In 1905, shortly before the opening of the Douma, Mr. Stead made a tour of Russia on a stirring campaign on behalf of his ideal of "patriotic co-operation" on imperial lines—a dangerous flag to fly with a "Revolution" in process, and one which drew the fury of the revolutionaries down upon him. "But none the less," wrote Dr. Dillon, the special correspondent of the *Daily Telegraph* in St. Petersburg, "Russians were favourably impressed by the spectacle of this apostolic reformer come from the distant shores of Britain to preach the gospel of modernism to the Russian *mooshik*" and even the enemy were "struck by his mysterious power of arousing sympathy and grasping the heart and the conscience of his hearers."[23]

Whether or not Mr. Stead was guided by the Great Empress in his life-long passion for "the evolution of the soul of Russia," is for the reader to determine according to the extent to which he is in sympathy with

---

[22] M.P. for Russia.

[23] Dr. Dillon wrote of W.T. Stead in May 1912, in the memorial number of the *Review of Reviews*: "His end, like his life, was grandiose, heroic. The tidings, at once mournful and soul stirring, when flashed across the wires, evoked a heartfelt response from one end of Russia to the other. In the remotest towns his name is familiar. In parts of Finland it is a household word."

the idea. By what method, for instance, comes the answer to prayer? To what extent is "the ministry of angels" an actual reality, and of what does it consist? He would have asked you all these questions had you been discussing the "Catherine" problem with him.

I have lightly touched in briefest detail on some of these evidences of "Russian influence" of which his life was so full, in order to show how easy it was for him and for those in closest sympathy with him to realize that there was some driving force, some unseen power at work which constantly energized his Russian sympathies. That power called itself Catherine II of Russia, and whatever may or may not be the "evidential value" of these striking communications from the point of view of the determined sceptic, there is no doubt that they formed immensely interesting reading and that they were a frequent source of inspiration to W.T. Stead in his writings on the Eastern Question.

Here, for instance, is one of these communications, which came through Mr. Stead's hand in December 1908, the MS. of which he sent me, with the following letter—

"Will you ask Catherine to annotate this, and after it is done, please bring it up, typed out (three copies), as annotated, but not showing which are annotations and which are not. Work her annotations into the text.

"The trouble of writing this is that my own ideas are so strong that I am not passive enough. If Catherine wants to erase any or all of it do not hesitate to let her do so. Let her write freely with your hand. Your mind is a clean slate, mine is not."

It was perfectly true that my mind was, as he phrased it, a "clean slate" so far as the Balkan Question was concerned. That storm-centre of Eastern Europe represented to me then little more than a geographical district. The sundry comments and additions to Mr. Stead's script, duly written by "Catherine" through my hand, were certainly not the product of my own mind. On my returning the annotated MSS. to the Chief he replied, "I have fired off Catherine's letter," and next day the message, signed X, duly appeared, in the columns of the *Westminster Gazette* for December 12, 1908, under the heading "Austria and Turkey: a Warning Note from the Balkans": from "A Correspondent who is in touch with many and varied sources of information in Eastern Europe." It would not be easy, I imagine, to detect the annotations "worked into" the original script. Mr. Stead told me he had read it, intact, to an exalted official personage who had given it the seal of his approval.

The letter began by touching briefly on the situation in the Near East, which, though at the moment apparently peaceful, threatened serious developments before the end of the year. With subtle wisdom it was urged that time should be given, not only to allow the disintegrating forces to work their way beneath the apparently solid surface of the Austro-Hungarian Empire-Kingdom, but also to allow the peoples of the Balkan peninsula occasion to sink their own internal disputes and present a front of solid unity against any outside assault.

The annexation of Bosnia and Herzegovina was discussed adversely, but without animus. And the Slavs were again exhorted to preserve an attitude of patience, for in the fateful outcome of the future might not Austria-Hungary yet disappear into the "melting-pot" to reappear, flushed with fresh vigour, as "the Federation of the Danube"? A consummation devoutly to be wished, yet one which hasty and untoward action on the part of the Slavs might postpone indefinitely.

In particular Macedonia was warned of danger, clear to eyes able to descry the signs of coming storm. At any moment, in the strained condition of local affairs, the most trivial episode might bring about a general upheaval, so delaying the longed-for reunion of the Slavonic race. A moment so full of promise yet of portent is an unerring test of a people's instinct. The Slavs were therefore implored to hold their strength in reserve, to take "Patience and Unity" for their watchword, … "for the day will come!"

Regarding the foregoing and similar communications Mr. Stead commented to me on one occasion—

> "My chief objection or difficulty is that these ideas are all my ideas. She may have given them to me long ago. But the in sceptic would say they are 'stained glass' and that I impute to Catherine only my own notions. You might ask her about this and see what she says. I think she gives me her thoughts, but she dictates more verbally to you."

Again he wrote—

> "Here is quite a long message from Catherine who says, you will see, that it is all right but needs careful annotating. I wrote it with much difficulty. But as she once said (or Julia, I forget which) that I get it most correctly when I get it with the greatest difficulty, this may be right!"

"Stained glass" was a favourite metaphor he used to imply that such communications were coloured by the mind of the person through whom they were transmitted, as light passing through a painted window reflects the prevailing tints.

The flamboyant style and vigorous phraseology of the Catherine communications, whether through the Chief's hand or through mine, was considered singularly alike, more so, I may say, than in the case of almost any other of our autoscripts, though Julia was always more or less *vraisemblable*, certainly in essence always so. I remember the Chief's telling me that he had read aloud one of my Catherine messages to a certain distinguished general, without saying from whom it came. The latter, supposing it to be Mr. Stead's, remarked that it was "Some of the best *Stead-ese* he had ever heard in his life!" The Chief's triumphant retort, "Wrong, my dear sir! It is not me at all. It is Catherine of Russia!" would hardly enlighten him much, though, as he was an old friend of the Chief, perhaps it did!

The question as to the possible "reincarnation" of Catherine, having come up, he wrote me as follows—

> *"November 15.*
> "With regard to your doubts about re-incarnation and Christianity, I do not in the least see any antagonism between the two. The Last Judgment is obviously not the judgment that follows the dissolution of the body, but the completed probation of the soul."

As to how far Catherine had left behind her, with her physical body, her earthly characteristics in the "old unhappy far-back time" he said—

> "The idea of having Catherine as a Guide is a novel one! Julia is of my own religion and ethics, but Catherine is—Catherine!" And again: "If the lion and the lamb are to lie down together, surely the lamb must satisfy itself that the "carnivore" has turned vegetarian."

Catherine was naturally much in evidence while he was writing *The M.P. for Russia*. I told him that to me her life stood out as one of the most pathetic tragedies in history. He replied that he would write of her as a great idealist, "whose real life was one long dream of the destined greatness of the Slavonic race."

Another of those unique documents was Catherine's Manifesto to the Slavs, which appeared in the *Contemporary Review* for January

1909, under the title "The Arrival of the Slav." The story of its inception is as follows—

On December 4, 1908, Mr. Stead wrote me:

> "I want you to ask Catherine whether she would like to write an article which I would have to sign, this article to deal with the general ferment and prospect in the Near East. It has occurred to me I might adopt the form of saying: "Suppose the great Catherine still lived, with mature judgment and widened experience, how would she contemplate the transformation of the East and what would she do?" She might work in her dreams and make them strike home by interspersing them with shrewd reflections upon the actual political situation as she sees it and foresees it. You might ask her what she thinks of the idea, and whether she would prefer to write it with your hand or with mine.
>
> I think it would be a great thing to re-introduce her to magazine literature, don't you?"

Catherine immediately expressed not only her willingness but her anxiety to write the proposed article, with an alacrity that almost implied that the original suggestion had emanated from her august influence. It was ultimately decided that the article was to be written in three parts or sections, the first of which would be written by the Empress herself through the hand of Mr. Stead, and would give a survey of the Russia of her own day. The second was to be by his own unaided authorship, and would generally review and comment on the existing situation; while the third portion was to be made up of parts of different "Catherine" messages that had come through his hand and through mine, and which dealt extensively with the immediate and distant future of Slavonia.

"I am going on with Catherine's article," wrote the Chief by return. "Bunting will take it for the *Contemporary*, so that is all right." Next day he sent me the first part, saying:

> "I enclose you Catherine. I do not feel as if I had done her justice, but I have got the general idea right. Before you come up you might just ask her if she has a message before I go on to the second part."

Then, a day or two later, Catherine having made sundry further suggestions, he wrote:

"Here is the second instalment. I have written it with my own hand, trusting to the Empress to alter what she pleases. ..."

So the thrilling drama unfolded. Very shortly afterwards the article was completed and duly made its appearance in the *Contemporary Review*. The Chief wished it to appear over the signature "Catherine," but this the Editor revolted against, insisting that it must be signed W.T. Stead. I quote one or two characteristic paragraphs, without specifying the different sections written by the two automatists, nor the "connecting links" or annotations added by the source of our inspiration.

The article began by noting the proposed annexation of Bosnia and Herzegovina to the Austro-Hungarian Empire-Kingdom as being but one of many signs of the ripening of the Slavonic question, the gradual emergence of the Slavs from the position of political serfdom and subordination, and their establishment as the predominant race of Eastern Europe:—

"Of all the great races in Europe the Slavs have received the fewest favours from the fates. Providence has been to them a cruel step-mother. They have been cradled in adversity and reared in the midst of misfortunes which might well have broken their spirit. From century to century they have been the prey of conquerors, European and Asiatic. When, as in Russia, they were able to assert their independence of Tartar and Turk, they could only do so by submitting to an autocrat whose yoke was seldom easy and whose burden was never light. But for this Cinderella of Europe the light is arising in the darkness, and there are not lacking signs that in the future the despised kitchen maid may yet be 'the belle of the ball.'"

The three eighteenth-century rulers who have been accorded the title of Great, were next contrasted in the following words:—

"The work of Frederick was no haphazard business. Before an intellect somewhat limited, but singularly clear and definite even in its limitations, there stood the vision of Prussia, aggrandised and all-powerful. He conceived his kingdom in the realm of thought before he gave it shape on the plane of matter. But he was otherwise no idealist. A strong man, resolute and unscrupulous, he carved with bloody sword his way to his goal.

"Peter was a ruler of another order, as much vaster as Russia transcends Prussia. He waged war with elementals, as Thor waged ceaseless war with the giants of Jotunheim, giants of mud, giants of ice, giants of immense size and corresponding stupidity. He was a Titan of the Promethean type bearing fire from heaven wherewith to illumine the dark wilderness of Muscovy. He was a barbarian intoxicated with civilization, passionate to acquire it for his country, *because* it was his country. The world has not yet done him justice; perhaps it will never do full justice to the almost superhuman energy of Peter the Great. He was cruel, yes; but as a surgeon is cruel who, lacking proper surgical knives to perform inevitable operations hacks off gangrened limbs with a forester's axe. Peter had three ideals. He spent his life in the attempt to realize them. First, to compel his people to avail themselves of the apparatus of the material civilization of the West. Second, to open up to the inland Muscovites a way to the three seas. Third, to bring to the mind of the Russian boyar and the Russian moujik a sense of the position, the greatness, and the destiny of Russia. Throughout his work from first to last runs the clear purpose of a strong man, labouring might and main to fulfil his mission. Faults he had as great as his qualities; savage, cruel, call him what you will, yet he saw his duty and lived and died in doing it. His failures were more wonderful than the successes of his contemporaries, and he has carved his name in imperishable granite upon the history of Russia.

"Of the three monarchs designated Great in the eighteenth century by far the most interesting, and in many ways the most tragic, was Catherine the Second. Interesting because of her lofty ideals; tragic because of the lamentable destiny that seemed to mar her noblest purpose and blight her highest aspirations. There is a note of pathos throughout the whole of Catherine's life, a sense of vast discord that might have been resolved into the grandest harmonies had the hand of a master but touched the keys. ...

"In those dark days when she lived almost alone, the future Empress delighted to forget the uncongenial environment of the present in the glories of the past and in the still more far-reaching vistas of the future. But there grew up within her an unconquerable resolve to possess her soul in patience until the time should arrive when she would be able to give effect to the aspirations which flitted ghost-like before her, but which she dimly felt she was to clothe with the flesh and blood of realized fact. She waited but for Time and the Hour.

"When Catherine found herself Empress of Russia she exulted in the opportunity of attempting to realize the dreams of her suppressed girlhood, when in neglect and solitude she spent her days in tearing the heart out of the books which were her only companions."

The ideals which justly won for Catherine the title of Great were next touched on in a rapid survey.

"The first great dream of her life was to compel Russia to become civilized, as she understood civilization. France then stood at the head of the culture and humanity of the world, and she became passionately devoted to the French philosophers, corresponded with them and promoted the circulation of their works among her people. They were perhaps but poor leaders and guides, but they were the most conspicuous lights of her time. Peter had introduced his subjects to the material civilization of the West. It was Catherine's ambition to supplement and complete his work by introducing to the nation the laws, the learning, and the arts of the West. Her court became the centre of whatever there was of culture in Muscovy. She wished to educate her people, and she was as zealous for the education of women as of men.

"Her second aspiration was to free Russia finally from the last vestige of Asiatic domination. Hence her wars, which gave Russia the seaboard on the Euxine and planted the Russian standard beyond the doorway of the Caucasus.

"Herself a German, she nevertheless appreciated keenly the distinctive genius of the Slavonic race. Russia, the first of the Slavs to become independent, the first also as she fondly believed to become cultured, was in her eyes destined to achieve a great historic mission. Russia was to be the elder brother of all the Slavs, the deliverer and the helper of the younger races. Nor was that all. In her more exalted moments she dreamed of making the Slav the link between two continents, the mediator between Europe and Asia, the great bridge between East and West. Towards this end she laboured, often with but little wisdom, but with unswerving instinct. She was baffled by the unfitness of her instruments and the inadequacy of her resources. But despite all disappointments Catherine, judged by her aspirations and even by the comparative success with which she began their realization, will always rank as one of the greatest rulers of the world. Only now, in our own day, when the Slavs are awakened all along the line, do men begin to see not only the greatness and the glory of her ideal, but the possibility of its realization on the lines which she laid down."

The article concluded with a confident assurance to the Slavonic people of the grandeur of their destiny, and an impassioned entreaty to them to possess their souls in patience for a time. In latter developments in the Balkan war surely one may see the fruits of the disregard of that far-seeing counsel.

"The day of cast-iron Empires is fast drawing to a close. The new century begins the era of decentralization and federation. In one form or another the whole vast stretch of country from Petersburg to Prague, from Prague to Adrianople, will be covered by a federation or federations of self-governing States, as peaceful as the Swiss cantons, in which the Slavs, by sheer force of numbers, will of necessity be in the ascendant. Nor will it be surprising if the despairing effort of the German to stem the tide of destiny in Poland, should lead to the addition of the German Polish lands to the federation of the future.

"The chief danger, almost the only serious danger, that threatens to retard the inevitable triumph, is the fatal tendency to anarchy that has ever been the bane of the Slavonian peoples. It was this that ruined Poland. It may postpone indefinitely the coming of the Slav into his kingdom. If we had the tongues of men and of angels we would cry aloud in the ears of all the Slavonian peoples: 'In unity is your strength. United you can conquer all your foes. Disunited you will remain the despised and impotent thralls of your neighbours. Peace! Peace among yourselves! Patience and Unity. By those watchwards you will conquer.

"If these counsels prevail, then the good seed which Catherine sowed in the dark days of storm and tempest may spring up and ripen for the glorious golden harvest. Then may be fulfilled her majestic vision of the advent of the mighty kingdom of Slavonia, which will represent more than the splendour of ancient Rome; more than the vainly desired perfection of classic Hellas."[24]

---

[24] I have to thank the Editor of the *Contemporary Review* for his kind permission to quote so extensively from *The Arrival of the Slav*. E. K. H.

12

"How I Know The Dead Return"

~

OLD LETTERS AND MEMORANDA SHOW the autumn of 1908 to have been one of unusual psychic activity for Mr. Stead and for some of those most immediately in touch with him. Along with the development of the "Catherine" drama came the greater urgency of Julia's appeals for the establishment of her "Bureau" which she declared must be delayed no longer. Through the Chief's hand she continued to write to this effect more insistently than ever. At intervals, for several weeks, a vigorous discussion as to ways and means was maintained between these two ardent souls, the one in the Seen, the other in the Unseen. Mr. Stead protested that Julia's plan was "impossible," that he had not time in which to devote himself to the project, and that even if he had the time he had not the money. To all this, Julia replied with finality: "You will get the money, and when it comes you will have no doubt about its being intended for my Bureau!"

He continued to protest: "Julia, it is no good settling such a task on me. I am such a poor instrument. It will certainly fail." To this she replied, with supreme confidence: "No doubt it might, if *you* were managing the Bureau. But it is I who shall manage it, and I assure you it will not fail."

He reminded Julia that it could not be done under a thousand pounds a year. Julia immediately wrote: "You will get the thousand pounds; you will hear of it before Christmas; and it will come from America.

I do not see many things of which you ask me, but I do see that. And you will see that it will all come true, just as I have said."

Such, in effect, is the substance of the messages which were received by the Chief through his automatic hand during the autumn of 1908. They have been carefully preserved in his psychic archives. I have dwelt upon this part of the story of the Bureau because, as a "concrete example"—as he called it—of a prediction fulfilled to the letter, it is one of the best on record. When commenting to me upon these messages he wrote: "I shall indeed regard adequate financial provision as a substantial sign of my duty!"

For my own part, I remember venturing to suggest some misgivings as to the wisdom of asking otherworld advice on matters of finance. But the Chief only replied with characteristic decision, "With regard to financial matters, the test is the fulfilment of their prophecies!"

He argued that as our sojourn on the earth is for purposes of spiritual development, such development can best be helped by whatever tends to guide us safely through the tangled maze of physical life. By helping us with their clearer vision, and without impairing the exercise of our own volition, our friends in the higher plane of being are but acting as missionaries or ministering angels. He quoted Sir Oliver Lodge: "Is it not legitimate to ask ... whether if an opportunity of service to brethren arises, an effort to seize it may not be made even by a saint?"

On December 14, the first anniversary of his son's death, he received a number of friends at his house at Westminster and spoke much of his hope to realize his cherished wish, to found "the Bureau." It was a Sunday afternoon. No sign of sadness was on his face, nor in his voice; only a joyous serenity as though reflecting the inward consciousness of "the light that never was on sea or land."

His friend Dr. Abraham Wallace, speaking long afterwards at a meeting of the London Spiritualist Alliance, alluded to that day, and to the beautiful example "not only of belief but of conviction as to the continued functioning of friends on 'the other side,' afforded by the speech Mr. Stead made on the passing of his son William. He felt that his work was being carried on with the assistance of that beautiful spirit. Such was the consolation experienced by a true spiritualist."

A vivid contrast, this attitude of mind, with that of Matthew Arnold, whom a friend found soon after the death of a dearly-loved relative, seeking consolation in the cold philosophy of Marcus Aurelius.

In this spirit, then, Mr. Stead conceived his unique ministry of service to the bereaved. It was the reason, pure and simple, for which he founded Julia's Bureau, that others whom death had made desolate should realize, as he had done, that:

> "There is no death, what seems so is transition;
> This life of mortal breath
> Is but the suburb of the Life Elysian
> Whose portals men call death."

During December, 1908, the Chief felt impressed to write an article entitled "How I know the Dead Return,"[25] some personal experiences that had "dispelled all doubt in his mind as to the reality of a future life." It began:

"Cecil Rhodes once told me that early in life he had devoted much thought to the question whether or not there was a God. He came to the conclusion that there was a 50 percent, chance that there was a God, and therefore that it was a matter of the first importance to ascertain what God wanted him to do. In like fashion I would ask the reader to consider whether or not there is any proof that the conscious life of his personality will persist after death. If he examines the evidence he will probably come to the conclusion that there is a certain percent, chance that such is the case. He may put it at 50 percent., at 90 percent., at 10 percent., or even at one percent, offchance that death does not end all. In face of the fact that the immense majority of the greatest minds in all ages have firmly believed that the personality survives death, he will hardly venture to maintain that he is justified in asserting that there is not even a one percent, chance that he will go on living after his body has returned to its elements.

"Of course if he should be absolutely convinced that not even such an irreducible minimum of a chance exists that he may be mistaken; if he thinks that he knows he is right, and that Plato and the Apostle Paul are wrong; I beg him to read no further. This article is not written for him. I am addressing myself solely to those who are willing to admit that there is at least an off chance that all the religions and most of the philosophies to say nothing of the universal instinct of the human race may have had some foundation for the conviction that there is a life after death. Put the percentage of probability as low as you like, if there be even the smallest chance of its truth it is surely an obvious

---

[25] December 18, 1913.

corollary from such an admission that there is no subject more worthy careful and scientific examination. Is it a fact, or is it not? How can we arrive at certainty on the subject? It may be that this is impossible. But we ought not to despair of arriving at some definite solution of the question one way or the other, until we have exhausted all the facilities for investigation at our disposal. Nothing can be less scientific than to ignore the subject and to go on living from day to day in complete uncertainty whether we are entities which dissolve like the morning mist when our bodies die, or whether we are destined to go on living after the change we call death.

"Assuming that I carry the reader thus far with me, I proceed to ask what kind of evidence can be produced to justify the acceptance of a belief in the persistence of personality after death, not as a mere hypothesis, but as an ascertained and demonstrable fact.

"There are many kinds of evidence to which I only refer to avoid the imputation of having ignored them, because I propose to confine myself exclusively to the one description of evidence which seems to me the most convincing."

After touching upon the difficulties and uncertainties attendant on the receiving of communications from the Beyond, he proceeded to describe the various types of evidence received by himself, beginning with the first proofs of identity that had been given by Julia Ames. Regarding the objection of "telepathy" so often adduced by investigators, he said:

"There is one class of messages for which telepathy from incarnate minds, conscious or unconscious, cannot account. That is the class of messages which relate neither to past nor present events, but which foretell an event or events which have still to happen."

For evidence he quoted the following case in his own experience:

"Some years ago I had in my employment a lady of remarkable talent but of a very uncertain temper and of anything but robust health. She became so difficult that one January I was seriously thinking of parting with her, when Julia wrote with my hand, 'Be very patient with E. M.; she is coming over to our side before the end of the year.' I was rather startled, for there was nothing to make me think that she was likely to die. I said nothing about the message, and continued her in my employ. It was, I think, about January 15 or 16 when the warning was given.

"It was repeated in February, March, April, May and June, each time the passage being written as a kind of reminder in the body of a longer communication about other matters. 'Remember E. M. is going to pass over before the end of the year.' In July E. M. inadvertently swallowed a tack. It lodged in her appendix and she became dangerously ill. The two doctors by whom she was attended did not expect her to recover. When Julia was writing with my hand I remarked, 'I suppose this is what you foresaw when you predicted E. M. would pass over.' To my infinite surprise she wrote, 'No; she will get better of this, but all the same she will pass over before the year is out.' E. M. did recover suddenly, to the great amazement of the doctors, and was soon doing her usual work. In August, in September, in October, and in November, the warning of her approaching death was each month communicated through my hand. In December E. M. fell ill with influenza. 'so it was this,' I remarked to Julia, 'that you foresaw.' Again I was destined to be surprised, for Julia wrote: 'No, she will not come over here naturally. But she will come before the year is out.' I was alarmed, but I was told I could not prevent it. Christmas came. E. M. was very ill. But the old year passed and she was still alive.

'You see, you were wrong,' I said to Julia, 'E. M. is still alive.' Julia replied, 'I may be a few days out, but what I said is true.'

"About January 10 Julia wrote to me, 'You are going to see E. M. tomorrow. Bid her farewell. Make all necessary arrangements. You will never see her again on earth.' I went to see her. She was feverish, coughed badly, and was expecting to be taken to a Nursing Hospital where she could receive better attention. All the time I was with her she talked of what she was going to do to carry out her work. When I bade her goodbye I still wondered if Julia was not mistaken.

"Two days after, I received a telegram informing me that E. M. had thrown herself out of a four-storey window in delirium, and had been picked up dead. It was within a day or two of the end of the twelve months since the first warning was given.

"This narrative can be proved by the manuscript of the original messages, and by the signed statements of my two secretaries, to whom, under the seal of secrecy, I had communicated the warnings of Julia. No better substantiated case of prevision written down at the time, and that not once but twelve times, is on record. However you may account for it, telepathy, conscious or unconscious, breaks down here."

The lady whose tragic death occurred as related above, had during her lifetime been somewhat of a sceptic, but she had promised Mr. Stead that if she should die before he did, she would try to do four very definite things, in proof of her continued existence. What these four things were, and how his friend carried out her intentions, Mr. Stead related as follows:

"She had constantly written automatically with my hand during her life. She promised in the first place that if she could she would use my hand after death, to tell me how it fared with her on the other side. In the second place she promised that if she could she would appear to one or more of her friends to whom she could show herself. In the third place she would come to be photographed. And fourthly she would send me a message through a medium, authenticating the message by countersigning it with the simple mathematical figure of a cross within a circle.

"E. M. did all four.

"(1) She has repeatedly written with my hand, apparently finding it just as easy to use my hand now as she did when still in the body.

"(2) She has repeatedly appeared to two friends of mine, one a woman, the other a man. She appeared once in a dining-room full of people. She passed unseen by any but her friend, who declares that she saw her distinctly. On another occasion she appeared in the street in broad daylight, walked for a little distance, and then vanished. I may say that her appearance was so original that it would be difficult to mistake her for any one else.

"(3) She has been photographed at least half a dozen times after her death. All her portraits are plainly recognizable, but none of them are copies of any photographs taken in earth life.

"(4) There remains the test of the message accompanied by the sign of the cross within a circle. I did not get this for several months. I had almost given up hope, when one day a medium, who was lunching with a friend of mine, received it on the first attempt she made at automatic writing.

'Tell William not to blame me for what I did. I could not help myself,' was the message. Then came a plainly but roughly drawn circle, and inside it a cross. No one knew of our agreement as to the test but myself. I did not know the medium, I was not present, nor was my friend expecting any message from E. M.

"Is it surprising, then, that after such experiences I have no more doubt of the possibility of communicating with the so-called dead, than I have of being able to send this article to the Editor of the *Fortnightly Review?*"

The friend to whom Mr. Stead refers in paragraph 4 of the foregoing narrative was Miss E. Katharine Bates, who has herself told the story with fuller details in her book, *Seen and Unseen.* It was in the presence of Miss Bates that E. M. wrote her name and message and the prearranged sign, The psychic through whose hand E. M. so convincingly communicated was, says Miss Bates, the well-known non-professional sensitive Miss Rowan Vincent.

Then followed an account of the well-known "Piet Botha "photograph incident,[26] and the article proceeded:

"What is wanted is that those who profess to disbelieve in the existence of life after death should honestly attempt to define the kind of evidence which they would consider convincing. I have narrated in this paper what seems to me conclusive evidence of the continuance of personality after death. All these incidents occurred in my own personal experience. Their credibility, to my readers, depends upon their estimate of my veracity. These things actually occurred as I have written them down. Supposing that they had happened to you, my reader, could you refuse to admit that there is at least a prima facie case for a careful exhaustive scientific examination into the subject? What more evidence, what kind of evidence, under what conditions, is wanted, before conviction is established?

"I ask no one to accept anything on other people's testimony. It is true that all people are not mediums, any more than all telephones can take Marconi messages. I am fortunate in being my own medium, which eliminates one possible hypothesis. But there are plenty of honest mediums, some possibly in your own family, if you cared to see them."

In some touching words he spoke of his son's passing, and what it had meant to him to receive his boy's messages of consolation and affection.

"No one could deceive me," he concluded, "by the fabrication of spurious messages from my son. Twelve months have now passed, in almost every week of which I have been comforted and cheered by messages from my boy, who is nearer and dearer to me than ever before. ...

---

[26] See "My Father," by Estelle W. Stead, pp. 267-71.

"After this I can doubt no more. For me the problem is solved, the truth is established, and I am glad to have this opportunity of testifying publicly to all the world that, so far as I am concerned, doubt on this subject is henceforth impossible."

On December 6 he forwarded me the MS. of the article to read and annotate, remarking—

"I think my article rather an important manifesto. Ask Julia and Willie whether they have any corrections or additions to make. Also where they think it should be printed. My fingers are all right, but I am a bit tired."

The reference to his fingers is explained by his letter of two days before. He had become very much interested in what is popularly termed "new thought" in special relation to healing, and about that time he wrote several articles on the subject after having heard the views of the leading exponents of Christian Science and kindred theories.

Hence the following (4 December, 1908):

"Tonight I got three fingers jammed in a taxi-cab so badly that I thought the bones would be broken and that at any rate they would swell and I would not write for days. I 'treated' them, and in three minutes all the pain had gone."

The article "How I know the Dead Return" duly appeared in the *Fortnightly Review* for January, 1909. It was also published in the *New York American*, later it appeared in Australia, in India, and also in *La Revue*, Paris. A few months afterwards it was published in volume form by the "Ball Publishing Company" of Boston, U.S.A.

When I went into Mowbray House on the morning of Christmas Eve Mr. Stead met me with a radiant face and the announcement: "The crisis of my destiny has arrived! Hearst has just sent to ask me to do special correspondence at £500 a year. Julia says this is the signpost. She says I must accept Hearst's offer, but I have to ask £1000, and what is more she says I will get it!"

Who could help being thrilled by such tidings! How vividly the scene comes back to memory! The familiar old "Sanctum," with its book-lined walls and innumerable photographs; outside, nothing visible save the yellow December fog, lying low on the Embankment; inside, the grey-bearded dreamer with the heart of a child and the brain that "thought for nations" pacing up and down the room, both hands thrust deep into his pockets, rapidly sketching his dazzling plans for "the intercommunion of the two worlds" and diffusing the irresistible magnetism of his own radiant faith. Who could look into those clear blue eyes without feeling that he saw further into the mystery of Being than most men see?

When I left him I had no more doubt that Julia's confident assurance would come true than had my Chief himself. ...

> "I enclose Julia's letter about the Bureau. Is it not very definite and decisive! she evidently has no doubt about it," he wrote on December 27.—"thinks I ought not to use the American money for the Bureau. But I do not agree. I shall not abandon what Julia calls the 'vantage' of the position that the money is given to me for the Bureau, that is, if it is given, of which as yet I have no information. I do not know when the answer will come one way or the other, but when it comes I shall let you know at once. ... I am trying to do the Book of the Month as a foreword for the Bureau."

His letters for the following week or two palpitate with keen anticipation, with only now and then a little half-impatient "aside" in parenthesis "Still no word from New York!"

New Year's Day came and went, without further "signpost" of any kind. He wrote me a New Year's greeting, full of the touching recognition with which he more than repaid one's least efforts to carry out his wishes; full, too, of his consciousness of the nearness of the cloud of witnesses.

Then, for the first time, he wrote doubtfully on January 5:

> "At present we have 'put our fortune to the touch, to win or lose it all.'
> If the money does not come!"

Another fortnight passed. Still no news from America. I must confess there were moments when my own faith grew faint and I wondered secretly whether the Chief had "dropped the substance for the shadow." But the slightest hint of such misgiving only brought the taunt "You are a perverse little mis-believer!" so I said no more. "No word from New York yet," he wrote again in the middle of January, adding hopefully, "But Julia says it will be all right!"

The third week in January he went down to Holly Bush, his seaside cottage at Hayling Island, to revise the last proofs of *The M.P. for Russia*.

As evidence of Julia's serene and unbroken assurance he wrote soon after his arrival, "Julia has just written a long direction for the organizing of the Bureau. ... I am now going to stick to proofreading!"

He lost no opportunity of taking "cross-messages" in auto-writing about subjects of the moment, and the result was an interesting array of experiments in telepathy. Regarding one such attempt between us he wrote on January 18:

> "I think you and everyone else will be struck by the absolute identity of thought and information and of style in each of the two pairs of messages.
>
> "I have been re-reading Julia, with your annotations. Julia's Letters will be the Thomas-a-Kempis *Imitation* of the new century. They are much more adapted to the temper and needs of the times."

So things went on, till one day, 19th January, when I had almost ceased to look for news, I received a telegram from my Chief, brief but eloquent:

"Sing Doxology. Julia's prophecy fulfilled"—and at night came a big bundle of O.K. proofs, and a note brimming over with joy:

> "Is it not splendid! Julia's prophecy has been fulfilled. The American has accepted my offer. Julia's Bureau, with C. House and M. House, is now secured. I have no time for more; I am coming up tonight to get off my first Letter. Now I must stop. I feel like singing the Doxology!"

So he rejoiced; not because of added means of luxury for himself, but because of added power to earn by the work of an already highly-taxed brain the means of opening the door to "more light" for those who groped their way through shadows.

13

Mecca and Medina

~

THE INTERVAL BETWEEN THE FULFILMENT of Julia's prophecy, as told in the last chapter, and the opening of her Bureau, to be related in the next, remains in my mind as a series of cinematographic pictures, viewed through the atmosphere of buoyant anticipation in which our Chief perpetually lived. In order to interest me in the forthcoming routine work of the Bureau, for which I was to act as secretary on his behalf, he was kind enough to give me many opportunities of being present with him at séances with the various psychics whose gifts he was never weary of putting to the test. He investigated different; forms of "mediumship" with the same ardent and patient spirit in which an astronomer studies the stars. He regarded "sensitives" as beings endowed far above their fellows, with a gift mysterious because so little understood, a gift which promised the evolution of another sense as yet rudimentary in the race as a whole, as the sense of taste was rudimentary in the Cave Man. Fresh evidence of this sixth sense he sought wearilessly, year in and year out, as men seek after hidden treasure.

From these sentiments evolved his idea of dedicating Cambridge House to be the Inner Sanctuary of Julia's Bureau. It should be as a temple, or sacred fane, apart from "the madding crowd." Here, from time to time, sensitives should be invited to rest in its tree-shaded and flower-fragrant peace, that their gifts might have fit opportunity to manifest without let or hindrance. Formerly his residence for nearly thirty years, this house at Wimbledon must, the Chief felt, be ideal in its fitness for his best-loved work, the investigation of as much as God should will us to know, while still on our earthly pilgrimage towards the "Land of Light." Here he had pondered over some of his finest inspirations. "In that garden," he once told me, "it was suddenly borne in upon me that I had to write the 'Maiden Tribute.' On a glorious Spring morning the full horror of the whole thing burst upon me. It seemed to blot out the blue sky and the sunshine, and silence the song of the birds. I wondered how the sun could shine, and how it was God did not blot out the whole world. Here in the garden were only the peace and beauty of nature, and yonder, in the great city, was Hell!" . . .

The "Borderland Library," his collection of psychic books, was to be kept at Mowbray House, from which the active ministry of the Bureau was to be conducted. The offices of the *Review of Reviews* were shortly to be transferred to new premises at Bank Buildings, Kingsway, so that he might have the editorial and publishing departments under one roof. But he had retained several rooms at Mowbray House, including his own old Sanctum, to be the head-quarters of the "Great Emprize."

"Cambridge House will be the Mecca, and Mowbray House the Medina, the sacred places of the New Revelation," he wrote in the terms of glowing metaphor so natural to him.

It has often been written of him that he was "so gullible" and that he did his psychic work in a wholly unscientific manner. Now, the truth is that he had a thorough method in all he undertook to do. Careful notes were always made of every phenomenon and manifestation, not only by himself, but frequently at his request by each sitter who was present on the occasion. A record of all sittings was kept, whether of Julia's "Inner Circle" at Cambridge House, or of others at Mowbray House or with psychics at their own homes. The notes were carefully written out within a few hours, dated, docketed, and placed in the Archives, and the "pros and cons" of each one carefully considered on its own merits, without prejudice. It would be invidious to mention all the sensitives so tested, they were very numerous, and of many nationalities, and varying degrees of development. The results in some cases were far from satisfactory, in others quite beyond question in their clear evidence and freedom from suggestion of fraud. Our Chief seemed, no doubt, to wear "his heart on his sleeve" where psychics were concerned, but beneath all this bonhomie was a power of acute discrimination, of keen insight, and the instinct to weed out the false from the true. But what are known as "psychical research" methods were abhorrent to him. He held them truly "unscientific" in the most extended meaning of the word. He said he would rather "die in the workhouse" than believe that anyone would tell him a deliberate falsehood, for the mere purpose of deceiving him. But, equally, he balanced results with one another, and took them for what they were worth in their ultimate. I well remember the scorn with which he told me of someone to whom he had lent a large sum of money, and who failed to return it at the time promised, indeed never returned it at all, but who said in extenuation: "Well, Mr. Stead, I could easily have left the country, but you see I haven't done so!"

"That speech," said the Chief, "was what really turned me against him! If he were really in such low water that he could not fulfil his promise to me, that was his misfortune, and I could sympathize. But when he seemed to expect me to admire him because he *might* have bolted and *didn't*, that was really too much!"

That he "rushed everywhere after mediums and swallowed everything he was told by them" is one of the glib mis-statements that have been repeated with parrot-like persistence by those who either knew him only superficially or did not know him at all. Let it be granted that this popular error was to some extent, to outward appearances, justified, because he had the journalistic instinct so strongly developed that after a certain point a subject ceased to be, with him, merely a matter for private investigation but became a theme for public discussion. Knowledge, however imperfect or rudimentary, concerning matters which he believed to involve the interests of the human race, he held to be an eternal prerogative, one of the supreme Rights of Man. By conviction he was democratic, and in nothing was this more evident than in his love of free and open discussion, whether the subject were a coal strike or a super-physical manifestation. In matters psychic as in all else he consulted everybody within reach, discarnate as well as incarnate, but did exactly as he pleased, or, as he would say, he always followed "his own signposts," To ventilate a matter by hearing a number of different views upon it, was, in his opinion, the best way of arriving at an unbiassed conclusion. Even with regard to mental and spiritual gifts, as with all other advantages, he held it a duty to "share with another's need." Just as he said "Every *wrong* is a divine call to you to take your share in trying to *right* it," and "Never founder a friendship; the more your friend fails you, the more he really needs you"; so he felt also "If God has put one in a niche from which one can see a few yards further ahead than some of the others, it is a plain duty to tell them what one sees."

"Ten frauds don't minimize one fact," was another of his favourite aphorisms, "any more than, if nine patients die, it follows that the doctor can't cure the tenth!"

I do not think there was ever anyone in his position so accessible as he, certainly none have been more accessible, either to psychics or any other variety of mankind. To what other editorial "sanctum sanctorum" could the passing wayfarer have demanded admittance and been given leave to enter, with the words "Mr. Stead is very busy, but he will see you in a few minutes"?

Could anything be more characteristic than the following story, which recurs to me at the moment. Some of us had besought him to deny himself to the general public at least on the day of "going to press" usually the last day of each month, for the time which was then snatched by callers had often to be made up by him at home in writing far on into the night. He reluctantly agreed, but his good resolution was in this respect an amusing failure. It so happened that, while he was deep in the midst of an article, he was told that a Mr.—— had called and was most anxious to see him for a very few moments on important business. Now Mr. Stead happened to remember that —— was the name of one of his provincial Helpers, and the Helpers were understood to be welcome at the office whenever they happened to be passing through London. So he laid down his pen (he was not on that occasion dictating the article) and went out into the waiting room with outstretched hand, only to find that his visitor was not the Mr. he had supposed, but a stranger of somewhat shabby aspect, whose opening sentences proclaimed the nature of his mission:

"Mr. Stead, I am on my way to Edinburgh, where a good and permanent situation awaits me. But I am in the meantime totally without means to get myself a dinner. As I was passing through London it occurred to me to call and ask if you would take pity on me and lend me half-a-crown for that purpose. I will return it to you as soon as I get to Edinburgh, without fail."

"My dear sir," replied the Chief, his eyes twinkling, as he took in the situation, "as London happens to contain nearly seven million units, may I ask why you have done me the honour of selecting me as the particular unit to provide you with a dinner?"

"Because, Mr. Stead, you believe in the union of all who love in the service of all who suffer, and I have had nothing to eat since yesterday. I assure you on my word of honour you need have no doubt of my returning you the money."

"For the sake of your word of honour I hope that you *will*" returned Mr. Stead as he dived into his pocket ("just to get rid of the poor chap!" he said apologetically afterwards), but let me tell you, you will be the first who has ever done so!"

The stranger departed, filling the air with his blessings. Perhaps he never reached Edinburgh after all. At any rate Mr. Stead never heard of him again.

In the old days at the *Pall Mall Gazette* office in Northumberland Street, a notice hung at the foot of the stairs, stating the hours during which the editor would be visible, and adding "As time is short and callers are many, the latter are requested not to waste the former." But no such warning guarded the portals at Mowbray House or Bank Buildings, where there was "Open Sesame" for all, and visitors from every land came and went as they listed.

The early spring of 1909 was altogether a strenuous time, or perhaps I should say a super-strenuous, for all his days and weeks were a never-ending stream of indescribable activity. He was editing the *Review of Reviews*, reviewing books, writing articles, interviewing people, carrying on a large uninterrupted private correspondence with his hosts of friends (correspondence which amply takes the place of a regular diary, which he never kept), going hither and thither on political and other missions connected with his work, and above all as he himself placed it keeping in daily touch with "the Invisibles" through his automatic hand.

Early in February he went down to Hayling Island, to think out his plans for the Bureau, and to get a little rest. In accordance with his invariable habit of utilizing every spare moment he often wrote letters in the train or while waiting in railway stations, and among my letters from him I find the following:

"February 4, HAVANT (while waiting for the train).

"Here I am on my way to Hayling. I hope that when I return I may have the whole scheme for the Bureau worked out and that I may have Julia's new edition ready for the printer. Do you know I found on an old slate some writing which I got inside a closed slate at Chicago in 1894, a message from William Pitt!

"I had completely forgotten it, and only came upon it today. When Miss Earle got William Pitt I thought it was the first time he had ever come, and lo, he had announced himself and his sympathy with me 'in my work of Reform' fifteen years before!

"I shall go through the masses of auto-writing I have got here tomorrow, and read Julia's Life, which I have never read all through."[27]

Referring to a "message" someone had sent him, purporting to come from the late Dr. Kenealy, he added:

"Dr. Kenealy was the counsel for the Tichborne Claimant. I did not know him intimately. I met him once at West Hartlepool when an egg thrown at him hit me! He was M.P. for Stoke, a genius but very erratic."

"February 5.
"I am sorting up Julia's communications. Her 'Life'[28] is most interesting and gives a glowing account of a young and beautiful rosy-cheeked maiden who was worthy to be the Julia of the 'Letters.' ... I enclose you one or two things of old time which will interest you."

He frequently received through his own hand messages in which the communicator urged upon him the necessity of doing only such work as none but he could accomplish and leaving minor tasks to others. "Julia, you will see, finds me troubled with the burden of things to do, and the appallingly little time in which to do them," was his significant comment one day, in sending me a batch of such communications. He added: "I enclose you a lovely cutting from Le Matin about the Empress Catherine, that will probably make a tour of Europe better than anything else," An allusion to the long-contemplated "Peace Pilgrimage," which was another of his cherished dreams.

The Invisibles constantly admonished him to give up smoking; it was a taste he had acquired comparatively late in life. He always said he had found a good cigar "helped conversation along" in an interview, and though he declared he would give up smoking "some day," he never did. His personal tastes were simple and abstemious, and he had no "fads" in diet. Like Dr. Johnson he "enjoyed a wholesome dish of tea," and he liked it inordinately sweet, demanding four, five, and even six lumps of sugar, and maintaining that sugar "made muscle," He had also a great

---

[27] A Young Woman Journalist.
[28] Ibid.

penchant for cakes. In matters of dress he was indifferent to details, getting much attached to his old suits, and regretfully discarding them for new ones. He used to say new clothes made him feel "profoundly miserable." Mourning he never wore. This was emphasized in Mrs. Stead's letter, read aloud by Dr. Clifford at the Memorial Service: "There is no need to put on mourning; he never would," He never carried a walking-stick, nor wore gloves. But he had a strong sense of "colour," and incongruities of attire jarred upon him, when they did not amuse him.

I find a passing reference to some of our "cross messages" in one of his letters, dated 7th March.

> "This is splendidissimus! I asked Miss Y—— to write with my hand. She did, before your report arrived. I have just seen her and you were perfectly right. I was perfectly right except in one particular. But it is evident we are getting on to perfection.
>
> This is the best cross-checked thing we have done yet. She told me all about it before I read it to her."

In March he wrote another psychic article for the *Fortnightly Review* on the "Exploration of the Other World," and sent it to me with the dry comment:

> "I think the most of my readers will think me clean crazy. But if there is anything in it at all, this is sober sense."

Next day:

> "Julia's article is off to the *Fortnightly now*. I think it will stagger most people and raise a fearful outcry against me.
>
> "The *British Weekly* actually says—
>
> "'The more cautious leaders of the Psychical Society are careful to warn the public that its main object is as yet unattained. Telepathy and automatic writing are placed by the newer investigators on the same plane as mesmerism and hypnotism. They afford no proof whatever that the dead communicate with the living. It has not been shown that, in response to all the anxious inquiries by trained and honest-minded scientists, a single syllable has yet reached us from beyond the grave.'
>
> "What next, I wonder!"

At last *The M.P. for Russia*, two bulky volumes of "Reminiscences and Correspondence," saw the light. He sent me down a "bushel of Press cuttings" concerning it, on all of which he remarked philosophically: "So far as I can see, none of the Reviewers have read the Book!"

I was not at all philosophical, but on the contrary rather indignant. "The *Times* has a perfect beast of an article about the O.K. book," he announced one morning, when I arrived at Mowbray House. He was sitting at his table in the Sanctum, writing as he spoke, but he smiled and shook his head reprovingly over my reply one irreverent to the "Thunderer"; then he added: "This is for you," and rose, handing me the volume in which he had been writing. It was *The M.P. for Russia*, on the fly-leaf of which he had inscribed:

"To my Faithful Helper
To whose unwearied service
I owe the possibility of producing this
book,—Miss Harper,
With gratitude,
W.T. STEAD.
March 16, 1909."

14

Julia's Day

⁓

JULIA'S CIRCLE MET FOR THE first time at Cambridge House. It was an April day.[29] Bound up with its wonderful memories is the brightness of sunshine and the promise of Spring.

We met in the library—in old days Mr. Stead's study—a long room with two windows opening on to a balcony. From the balcony the view over the garden a wilderness of trees and away to the slope of Wimbledon Common, suggested a glimpse of a Highland glen. Through the open windows, that April afternoon, the song of thrush and blackbird mingled with the Chief's brief prayer that this work of faith and love should be blessed.

After praying, he read one of his favourite chapters from the Bible, and some messages in automatic writing. Miss Earle was the sensitive for that first Circle meeting, and through her as intermediary many of our unseen friends greeted us. There was a deep sense of peace, and one was conscious of the thinness of the veil between the Two Worlds.

One or two friends were present in addition to Julia's chosen group. One of the former, Mr. Henry Blackwell, a patient and careful student of all forms of psychic phenomena in England and America, took several photographs of the Circle both before and after the séance.[30]

---

[29] April 24, 1909.

[30] Unfortunately it has been found that none of the photographs are quite clear enough for reproduction when enlarged for illustration. In sending me copies

Afterwards we had tea downstairs. No ceremony was complete, in Mr. Stead's eyes, without that hospitable benediction. Again we were photographed by Mr. Blackwell, this time in a group beneath "Julia's Oak," at the end of the lawn.

Then we all went up to town by an early evening train. The Chief had invited the members of the Circle and a few friends—including Mr. A. P. Sinnett, the Theosophical leader and author to dine with him at the *First Avenue Hotel*, High Holborn.

In the train, on our way to Waterloo, I remember the conversation turned upon the various pains and penalties to which those who professed to hold "communion with departed spirits" rendered themselves liable, under some long-forgotten Act of George II, unearthed for our edification by our honorary treasurer, Mr. Serocold Skeels. The Chief said, with an anticipatory gleam in his eyes—

"Julia's Bureau would make a good test case. It is high time that Act was off the Statute Book!"

Then he fell to talking about prophecies and premonitions and insisted that the future held in store for him a violent death.

"Kicked to death by a mob, I think it is to be," he added with complacence, as though speaking of some high honour which awaited him. "It sounds rather disagreeable," he added reflectively, "but it won't be nearly so bad in reality. A bang in the face with a hob-nailed boot sounds rather sickening, but it will soon be over!"

At dinner someone drew Mr. Stead's attention to the circumstance that we were "thirteen at table." Mr. Skeels was the first to notice this, and he made the remark that the first to rise from the table was said to be the one on whom the fatal augury would take effect. In an undertone Mr. Skeels then added to Mrs. Harper, his right-hand neighbour, that he intended to make some excuse to be, himself, the first to leave his place, and so allay possible nervousness on the part of any of the other guests. But his kind intention was forestalled. The Chief had laughed indulgently; he was not in the least superstitious. Had he not carried about with him for days a five-pointed star *unwittingly*

Mr. Blackwell wrote, February 6, 1914, "You will see that Mr. 'sStead's face is slightly blurred although he has not moved. I pointed it out to him at the time, thinking it might be psychic, but he rather pooh-poohed it, and I thought no more about it. Two or three months ago he was giving me a message through Miss Earle, and suddenly he said, 'By the bye, you were quite right about that Bureau photograph. My son Willie has told me that he tried to show on my face.' The photograph had not been referred to, neither was I thinking of it."

upside-down—"without anything happening!" so he declared. Signs and omens were not for him! Dinner came to an end; coffee was served; and Mr. Skeels, doubtless with the conscientious determination that we should not rush blindly on our fate unwarned, was reading with due solemnity further selections from the George II Act—received I fear with unbecoming mirth—when suddenly we noticed that under cover of the buzz of our animated conversation the Chief had quietly risen from his place at the head of the table.

I note the little episode, not by way of upholding that deep-rooted superstition, but merely as yet one more indication of his scrupulous thought for others, even in the smallest details of life. It is yet another curious coincidence that, though nothing untoward took place within the allotted twelve months, yet W.T. Stead is the first of that cheery company, the first member of Julia's Circle, to cross the Border.

The day closed with another sitting, held in the Sanctum at Mowbray House and presided over by Miss McCreadie, the "Highland Seer." Other sensitives, of note in the psychic world, were in the circle, and we were in no wise lacking conclusive demonstrations of the presence of the Invisibles. In all the world I do not think there was a happier man that night than our Chief. He had realized his most cherished hope.

Julia

Hullo

Catherine II (The Great)
Empress of Russia,
1762 to 1796.

Miss Harper

The Sanctum, Mowbray House

In memory Novem 10.1885
William T. Stead
Christmas 1911

10th November, 1885
Stead's 1911 Christmas card
(Prison clothes)

15

The Aeroplane

~

"We are each of us Spirits here in the mortal form."

FROM APRIL 24, 1909, AND onward for the first twelve months Julia's Circle met in the Sanctum at Mowbray House, every morning, except Sundays, at ten o'clock. Unless obliged to be absent on other business Mr. Stead was always present at those daily conferences with the unseen, in which he rejoiced. He arrived at Mowbray House soon after nine o'clock in the morning, and during the interval preceding the Service he was busily engaged in reading his enormous mass of correspondence ensconced in his favourite window-seat overlooking the river, with one leg tucked under him and an ever-increasing pile of letters, newspapers, torn envelopes and press cuttings scattered chaotically around him, but with their contents accurately stored for future reference in his mind. Occasionally a friend on opening the door would be greeted by a pellet of curled-up envelopes, if the mood of "Peter Pan" happened to be uppermost—the boy who wouldn't grow up! Very often he wrote one of his newspaper or magazine articles then, sometimes calling to me and suggesting asking the judgment of Julia or some other authority concerning some knotty point that arose. Seated in different rooms we consulted the oracle through our pens, and as often as not the opinion expressed through each was in substance the same. Doubtless the sceptic will say this does no more than prove an interesting example of thought-transference between two sympathetic minds. I do not offer it as an argument in favour of spirit return, but as an integral part of my recollections of Mr. Stead. I remember his delight when on one occasion, some debatable question having been referred to the Invisibles, Miss Scatcherd and Mr. Robert King, sitting in an adjoining room, obtained the same message in substance, if not worded the same, as that which came simultaneously to the Chief and myself through automatic writing in the Sanctum. It was a question relating to which of certain pictures should be selected for the Bureau, and in which of the rooms it should hang.

Our Chief was intensely fond of flowers, and the Sanctum was seldom or never without flowers of some kind. Now that it had become Julia's Bureau this was more than ever a necessity, and he often used to come in carrying a handful of violets or roses which he bought from the flower-sellers in the Strand, for most of whom he had a friendly greeting. And a regular toll of blossoms was exacted from the garden at Cambridge House all the year round.

"Julia must never be without flowers," he used to say. Another of his cherished acquisitions was a very large and sweet-toned polyphone which he bought from the psychic, Mr. Boursnell, shortly before the latter's death. It had a great variety of tunes and was allowed to play each morning for five or ten minutes before the sitting began. The members of the Circle were expected to arrive at Mowbray House two or three minutes before ten o'clock, and they frequently found the Chief rapidly penning the last lines of some fiery political manifesto destined to appear a few hours later in the columns of the *Westminster Gazette* or the *Daily Chronicle*—while the harmonious strains of "The Russian National Hymn," or "Ein' Feste Burg," rang from the instrument in the corner of the room. His power of *concentration* was phenomenal. It was not that the sounds themselves particularly appealed to him, but it was an axiom that music aided the blending of vibrations. So, if the spirit-friends wanted music, music they should have. Indeed I am not at all sure but that he sometimes martyrized himself in the matter, as he did in so many other things.

By Julia's direction the Service was conducted by each member of the Circle in turn. It began with prayer, which was followed by the reading and signing of the previous day's "minutes." After this, the applications for particulars as to the working of the Bureau, which began to pour in from all quarters of the globe, were passed in review. Automatic messages were read and discussed. Mr. Robert King was present each day from 10 till 1 for consultation. Clairvoyant and clairaudient to a high degree he had been introduced to Mr. Stead by Miss Scatcherd in the course of her own psychic investigations, and this had led to his engagement by Mr. Stead as the special clairvoyant for the Bureau. In Mr. King's absence Mr. A. Vout Peters acted as *locum tenens*. The latter was the psychic through whom General Gordon, twenty years after his passing, conversed with Mr. Stead, taking up the thread of their discourse from the point where it had been dropped before Gordon left England for the Soudan.

After a week or two Julia gave directions that the opening prayer should be followed by a short reading, "from one of the Bibles of the world." The selections chosen were more or less characteristic of the reader's own predilection, as, for instance, Mr. Stead nearly always read from the Old or New Testament, and if he were out of spirits he chose some psalm of particular jubilation, as a special rebuke to himself. Another member of the Circle, with Rosicrucian leanings, generally selected a passage from the mages, another inclined to Julia's Letters and the writings of Stainton Moses, yet another favoured Fenelon and the earlier mystics, while occasionally, though not in the case of Mr. Stead, who was never at a loss, inspiration in the choice of suitable readings sank to a low ebb, and the president for the day fell back ruefully upon one of those all too handy books of "selected daily quotations" which the Chief sarcastically dubbed the "refuge of despair!"

The sittings at Mowbray House were invariably held in broad daylight. There were no dark séances held in connection with Julia's Bureau, except those for the "direct voice" held two years later by Mrs. Etta Wriedt, at Cambridge House, and the best of these sometimes took place by daylight. The morning Circle sitting at Mowbray House must not be confused with the private sittings given to Bureau applicants. The "Morning Sitting" was for members of Julia's private Circle only, and strangers were never admitted, except in one or two rare instances, by Julia's permission. It was with no idea of forming a "clique" that this rule was maintained.

All students of occultism will understand the reason given by Julia herself. She explained that the daily meeting of the same group of sympathetic persons, chosen by herself, made a psychic focus of great and increasing power. It formed as it were a chalice for the "wine of inspiration," a pure light, vibrating along seven rays which met in mystic union.

The sudden introduction of a new element, however good in itself, said Julia, caused something equivalent to a fissure in the fine magnetic band that was being woven around the circle. Such is the occult explanation of Julia's reluctance to admit strangers to her Circle sittings.

For the first seven or eight weeks Mr. Stead presided at the morning meeting. Julia then wrote saying that it was to be conducted by each member in turn. As the Chief might have to be absent, she said, we must be prepared to act on our own initiative, when he was not with us. One wonders now, what deeper meaning underlay those words.

The Chief always prayed extempore, with the ease and fervour of a fine old Puritan. It was natural to him. Mr. King sometimes, not always, did the same. The rest of us generally resorted to the prayer written by Julia for the use of those who were, as the Chief said, so "lacking in grace" that they could not form a simple petition to the Almighty for a blessing on the day! Julia wrote her prayer through his hand, and it was printed afterwards in the pamphlet which explained the working of the Bureau.

Silence then reigned for a few moments. Then Mr. King, opening his "celestial ear," gave expression to the dominant influence. "I sense the presence of So-and-so," he would say, giving the purport of the message he was impressed to deliver. The Chief would take up the thread, and an animated discussion would follow.

As an example of one of these colloquies, which has the additional interest of a prophecy, speedily fulfilled, I quote the following. Mr. Stead wrote of it to *Le Matin*, and it was copied at the time by several English and Continental papers, but is probably new to many readers. It was given a day or two before Mr. Stead went to Châlons, to witness the first flight of M. Bolotoff's tri-plane. The interest of the message lay in the prophecy regarding this event:

"Mr. W.T. Stead relates in the *Matin* today a conversation with M. Lefevbre, the dead aviator, which he states took place at Julia's Bureau.

"The Members of Julia's Bureau meet every morning at ten o'clock, to confer with their directress, who, visible to the clairvoyant, occupies the presidential chair of the gathering. After having received two brief messages from Julia the clairvoyant said, 'I hear another voice speaking.' I now quote the following notes, taken down in the stenographer's notebook:

"'If you go to Châlons I will go with you.'

"Mr. Stead: 'Who is it that speaks?'

The Aeroplane

"Clairvoyant: 'I have been dead some time. My name is Lefevbre.'

"'strange as it may seem,' Mr. Stead here interpolates, 'this name awoke no memory in me. I was abroad when Lefevbre was killed, and I thought this might be someone who died a long while ago. None of those present recognized the name.'

"Another spirit began to speak, and the incident remained there. Next day Julia remarked in the course of her communications: 'That man, called Lefevbre, says that he will go with you to Châlons. He hopes you will go.'

"Mr. Stead: 'Ask Lefevbre if he was the man who was killed in the aeroplane accident?' '"Yes, I thought you knew it.'

"Mr. Stead: 'You can communicate directly with me? Do you understand English?' "Answer: 'No, not much; but I transmit my thoughts to the medium and he translates them into English.'

"Mr. Stead: 'What was it caused your rapid fall?'

"Answer: 'I did not have time to think. You scarcely have time to reflect when you fall.' "Mr. Stead: 'In your rapid fall did you keep your presence of mind?'

"Answer: 'This is what I felt. I was conscious that I was falling, but before touching the ground I had lost consciousness. I felt no pain nor any sensation in my physical body. It seemed to me that my spirit was projected out of it. I had a sensation of rapid rotation, then something gave way suddenly, and I found myself in the air, seeing beneath me my mortal remains and the machine. It was not disagreeable. I observed too that a being who was very powerful and who calmed me, was near me.'

"Lefevbre then asked Mr. Stead to warn M. Bolotoff, another aviator, at Châlons, *that his motor would not work properly.* Mr. Stead adds that he went to Châlons on the following Monday and warned M. Bolotoff of Lefevbre's advice. The motor was tested with extreme thoroughness and seemed in the most perfect order until M. Bolotoff took his seat in his aeroplane. Then the motor would not work, the starting handle broke, and the experiment had to be abandoned.

"Mr. Stead guarantees the accuracy of the above account which is confirmed by the shorthand notes and by the declaration of four or five persons who were present and heard the warning."[31]

Clairaudience through which the above message was received—is an extremely fine development of the Sixth Sense, whereby spirit-voices, inaudible to most, are at times perfectly audible to the sensitive so gifted.

---

[31] *Daily Mail,* 25 September, 1909.

16

The True Spiritualism

~

"THE GREAT MISSION OF SPIRITUALISM is to make A men spiritual."

These words were spoken by W.T. Stead in the Grand Theatre, Halifax, at the Spiritualists' National Union Convention, which met on July 4, 1909. He was asked to address the Convention, and though more than usually beset with work and engagements at the time, he accepted the invitation, feeling that an opportunity was probably given to him to offer some special words of guidance and counsel. He sought guidance for himself from his unfailing source, and the message given him to deliver lay in these words—"The great mission of Spiritualism is to make men spiritual."

How one wishes that every explorer of the "Land Psychic" would make them a St. Michael's sword, guarding the way.

The whole speech vibrates with the intensity of his convictions, as we who worked with him know full well.[32]

"MR. CHAIRMAN, LADIES AND GENTLEMEN,—
"I speak tonight with a sense of peculiar responsibility. I have given up public speaking, as the strain was more than I could stand in addition to my journalistic and other work. Tomorrow is my sixtieth

---

[32] Miss F. Scatcherd took a special, verbatim report of the address for *The Two Worlds*. By kind permission of the editor, Mr. J. J. Morse, I quote from it.

birthday, and I do not think I can end my fifty-ninth year better than by bearing my testimony to you, most of whom I have never seen before, and shall probably never see again, as to the words of truth that have proved my greatest help and inspiration.

"I was talking the other day to a distinguished statesman, a High Churchman, who said 'Religion depends chiefly in reliance upon the unseen.' If he be right, religion in this country is in a very bad way. Cecil Rhodes told me that whenever he met a Jew he always asked him if he ever heard in the synagogue any reference to a future life. He never met a Jew who gave an affirmative answer. I have applied the test to many churches. It is seldom you hear an expression of real faith in another world from any Christian pulpit, and very seldom any reference to ministering angels and spirits. The fact is, the Church has become practically materialistic. I hope that we possess in Spiritualism the means of a real revival in religion. But many Spiritualists are tinged with materialism; you do not like people to talk about religion, and I hope you will bear with me when I tell you I detect a materialistic note in many of your publications. Most of you are Atheistic the greater part of your time. You never can do wrong unless you cease to believe in God as a living force. We never can mourn or lament without having first lost faith in God. The great mission of Spiritualism is to make men spiritual. It is not the extension of materialism into the other world. That is a damnable error. The peculiar notion that Spiritualism teaches that there is no such thing as retribution for life lived in selfish neglect of the duties to God and humanity has no foundation; in fact, no spiritualist teaches an everlasting Hell. I do not think any religious man believes it.

"But behind the doctrine is an eternal truth. As a man leaves this world, so will he wake in the other world. You may find yourself in a state of utter, outer darkness, if you have lived a loveless, selfish life on earth.

"I remember David M'Cree, who was turned out of his church, saying to me: 'I do not object to Hell, I want to rehabilitate it.' Men have got rid of the idea that life here entails consequences hereafter.

"A friend of mine, a distinguished foreign lady, living in London, some time ago began to work the spirit indicator. She was only a beginner. Imagine her astonishment when the name of a great personage was spelt out. Slowly, letter by letter, he gave his name. And then in pathetic terms begged her to pray for him. 'Where are you?' asked my friend. 'In utter darkness, pray for me, pray for me.' He was not an exceptionally bad man, he had only lived a life of thoughtless indifference and self-indulgence. Soon after, he came again: 'Why have you not prayed for me; why have you not kept your word?' 'But I have prayed for you, in church, and all your countrymen, too, have prayed for you.' 'That matters nothing. I want, and must have, the fervent prayer of a loving soul.' 'But what is your condition?' 'I do not know, I am like a shipwrecked sailor, in darkness and loneliness, on an unknown shore. Oh, if you could only tell my relations of my experience it might help them to avoid my fate.' The same thing may wait for you and me. We think we are just men and women; in reality we are spirits spending a few years of education in this world which is but as a preparatory school for a larger life who in a few years will pass on to another state in which our position will be governed by the use we have made of our life here.

"I do not want any one present to be able to say that he stood within the range of the voice of W.T. Stead and that he did not warn him to flee from the wrath to come. But while it is necessary to say this, Spiritualism is at the same time one of the most beneficent agencies for interpreting the love of God."

He then went on to speak of the passing of his son, and declared that Spiritualism had stood the test of that terrible sorrow, and from it had taken the bitterness of Death. He spoke of the different ways in which his son had made his continued existence known to him, and added—

"I know my son would not care to come back to earth, that he is enjoying vistas of usefulness and ever-increasing knowledge that fill existence with increasing interest. Am I not bound to communicate to my fellows what has been such a joy to myself? Ought we to sit in our corner, contentedly munching our cake all to ourselves? Is that right? What answer can we make to our elder brother Christ, when He meets us and asks: 'What have you done for my other brethren?' You may say: 'Lord, I took in *The Two Worlds*, and read *Light*, and I went to the meetings when there was a specially interesting medium. ...' "I have been a journalist for forty years. I do not know a single leader-writer who warns his readers that they will have to answer for their actions in a world to come.

"... Some of you may believe Jesus Christ never existed. If He never did exist, then it is high time that someone set about realizing the ideal. Others of you share my belief that He exists as our leader to a better world. I will tell you about the beginning of my mediumistic career so far as I am a medium. When I was in Holloway Gaol one Christmas— you are all so busy catching trains and ringing up telephones, that you never have time to listen to the voice of your soul I had been trying to write a letter to a poor girl who had been rescued. She was finding the new life very dull and was in danger of falling back, and it was suggested that if I were to write to her it might have some influence over her for good.

"I left the letter unfinished to attend morning service, and was looking down from the organ loft on my six hundred fellow prisoners, when I heard a voice: 'Why are you telling that girl to be a Christian? Never tell anyone any more to be a Christian, always tell them to be a Christ.' "My mind revolted, and I said: 'What blasphemy!' But the voice went on: 'The word Christian has become a mere label, covering much of self, little of Christ.' "I pondered the matter deeply. I wrote to all those on whose judgment and spiritual insight I could rely to Cardinal Manning, to Hugh Price Hughes, to Josephine Butler, to Benjamin Waugh, and others. What would these spiritually-minded men and women think of it? With one exception all said: 'These words contain the essence of the Christian religion.' "Ever since then I have always passed on this message to my fellows. What does it mean? First, that you have to love all beings, not only the nice ones, the attractive ones, but those who seem less attractive, even repulsive. Secondly, you must sacrifice yourself for the well-being of others. Thirdly, you have to interpret the love of God to those around you. Each of you is the centre of a group of souls to whom, if you are not a Christ, perhaps no other interpreter of the love of God and the character of Christ may be sent.

"When you return to your home tonight you may be able to say a kindly word, or do a sympathetic action. And you do not speak that word, you do not perform the kindly deed. You are not a Christ. You speak the word, you show your sympathy by your actions, and you are a Christ to those persons. Even though you may call yourself an Atheist you are God's Christ to those people. ..."

He finished his speech on the buoyant note so characteristic of him—

"But my last word is not of warning, but of triumph. Christ came to bring not only peace; peace is a negative thing but joy, joy supreme in the absolute assurance that God is in His heaven, and that, therefore, all is right with the world."

An old friend of Mr. Stead, who was on the platform during the Meeting, writes:—

> "I shall never forget that speech, nor that loved face. ... People were stirred to their depths. He had been into the Unseen for his message and delivered what there he had won."

.

17

A Prophetic Message

INTERESTING AS IS THE EPISODE recorded in a previous chapter, in which the warning to an aviator was almost immediately fulfilled, yet it is not alone in our experience of fulfilled prophecies. Long before the aeroplane accident, which I told as relating more particularly to the Morning Circle, an equally definite warning was given, through another source, to Lady Warwick about her motor-car.

Three months after the opening of the Bureau, Mr. Stead wrote a brief, comprehensive summary of its progress. This appeared in the *International Magazine*, published in English, French, and German, and in the *Harbinger of Light*, an Australian paper, published in Melbourne, devoted to the study of psychology and occultism. It was published again in 1910 as a booklet, under the title *Bridging the River of Death*. The address quoted in the foregoing chapter was bound up in the same small volume, entitled *The Unseen World a Reality*.

In this article Mr. Stead referred to the second example of a warning prophecy mentioned above. It was a species of psychic communication to which he attached special importance, for it absolutely excludes telepathy as an explanatory theory, i.e. the class of messages relating to events unknown to any living person, events still in the future when the messages are received.

As the story has often been told, and has been much distorted in the telling, it seems well to relate it once more. And as I was one of those most immediately concerned in it, I am able to give the facts.

When sitting in the library at Cambridge House, on the evening of Whit Monday, 1909, my mother felt a strong impulse to place her hands on a small table. She called to me to join her, for she felt impressed that some unseen presence wished to communicate with us. At the moment she spoke I was playing an American organ near the farther end of the room. I finished the phrase, then came and sat with my mother at the table. Though I did not feel the influence of which she spoke, I had, a few moments before, noticed a small oval-shaped light, about the size of a large walnut and of a bright golden colour, travel swiftly across the library floor and disappear. It appeared to be an inch or two from the ground. I had watched it as I played. I have never seen a light exactly similar, neither before nor since. It was early in the evening, and the room was still in clear daylight. There was no one in that part of the house except ourselves. I may say that we were not much given to "table sittings," though like most psychic students we had experimented in that simple form of communication—the Morse code of the spirit world—at different times. But we did not incline to it, considering it a rather clumsy method of obtaining information which came with greater facility through automatic Writing, nor did we need our friends to move the furniture about in order to prove to us their continued existence, could they prove it otherwise. On the evening in question I felt no particular inclination to take messages at all, either in writing or in any other form, and it was more to please my mother than for any other reason that I acceded to her suggestion that we should "sit." I mention this, as it shows we were not in any sense "invoking the spirits," nor clamouring for communications from "the Other Side." We had spent the afternoon with friends in the neighbourhood, to whom matters psychic were *anathema*.

We had sat for some twenty minutes without any result, and were just thinking of giving it up, when suddenly the table began to tilt. It spelt out a man's Christian name, which I shall give here as N——. We had no friend of that name, therefore we asked why N—— had come. In answer, the table slowly spelt out the name of Lady Warwick. But there was nothing in the name of N—— to lead us to associate him with that lady. Indeed it had for us no association at all. So we did not feel we were much nearer. I knew nothing of Lady Warwick's movements, and had then only met her once. However, on asking whether N—— had a message for Lady Warwick the table rapped "Yes" the familiar three tilts then by the usual process of question and answer a message was rapped out, the table spelling each word letter by letter. The communication was short but very definite, begging Lady Warwick not to use her motor-car during the next week, saying in effect that if she did use it in that week she would have an accident and be run down. If she postponed her journey till the following week, no accident would happen. He then spelt "Send message," adding that he was a friend of Lady Warwick and that she would know from whom it had come.

I duly noted down the exact words of the communication at once, though I confess I did not take it very seriously. Next morning I took my notes to Mowbray House, and gave them to the Chief who had just returned that morning from Hayling Island, where he had been spending Whitsuntide. He said I ought at once to have transmitted the message to Lady Warwick, within a few minutes of receiving it. I replied that I had no idea from whom it had come, nor even whether such a person as the communicating spirit claimed to be, had ever existed. Also that I did not attach any importance to such "warnings." It was probably nonsense, and so forth, adding that but for my promise to inform him of all communications that came, I should have said nothing at all about it. Moreover, I remember saying that if I had sent it, and Lady Warwick had acted upon the warning and postponed motoring until the following week, no one could ever know whether the warning had been justified. The circumstance had for me no importance whatever. My mother was evidently much more open to impression in the matter than I, for it had been by her suggestion that we had "sat," and she had also been anxious that I should transmit the message to Mr. Stead and leave him to deal with it as he thought fit.

Mr. Stead immediately wrote to Lady Warwick, enclosing the message. His letter was posted between one and two o'clock on Whit Tuesday, within an hour or two after I had made it known to him. He heard nothing more till next day Wednesday evening about six o'clock, when to his joy he had a telegram from Lady Warwick saying that she had just received his letter, on her return to Easton Lodge, from which she had been absent since the previous day. She had left home on *Tuesday morning* Mr. Stead's letter had arrived on *Tuesday evening*; she however being absent had not received it till next day, Wednesday, when she returned. But, while driving through London on her way home on Wednesday afternoon, a motor-omnibus had turned the corner of the street on the wrong side of the road; the road being slippery and wet with rain the motor-bus "skidded," crashing into the rear of Lady

Warwick's car, and wrecking it completely. The remains of the car had to be left in London, and its occupants, in a more or less bruised and wounded condition after their narrow escape from death, took a cab to Liverpool Street station, whence Lady Warwick travelled home. On arrival she found Mr. Stead's letter containing the warning from N——,which had reached her just too late to prevent a catastrophe that might so easily have been fatal.

Meanwhile, we at Wimbledon remained in ignorance of the affair, and the startling sequel to the message, until next morning, Thursday, when I received a jubilant letter from my Chief, announcing it in these words:—

"You remember the N. message? Well!
"Lady Warwick's motor was smashed this afternoon by a motor-bus. She and her maid were flung out and motor smashed.
When she got home she found my letter with your message warning her to postpone her motor drive!
"Is it not *glorious*!
"I think she is almost pleased it happened because it confirms her faith!"

N—— was a friend of Lady Warwick. He had passed away some time before. When in this life he had promised to watch over her from the other side, should he be the first to leave this world.

Members of Lady Warwick's family and household gave corroborative testimony in regard to the accident, from their several points of knowledge, and those of Mr. Stead's staff to whom he mentioned the "warning" when forwarding it, confirmed the time at which his letter was written and despatched. The documents are all in order, without a single weak link in the chain of evidence.

When Mr. Stead quoted this case of prevision in *Bridging the River of Death*, it was thought better to tell it merely in outline, without giving any names. My mother and I had no wish for publicity, and our psychic experiments were then, as always, purely private. But the story spread, in various incorrect forms, and I am glad of this opportunity to give its full details for the first time, Lady Warwick having been good enough to permit me to mention her name.

So much were we interested in the result of our impromptu table séance, we from that time ceased to consider this method an inferior means of communication with those free from the body of flesh. No doubt, like the planchette, ouija-board, and similar contrivances, it may more easily lend itself to foolish and undesirable manifestations on the part of beings who dwell in the "lower levels," especially if the sitters are inexperienced, or sitting "for the fun of it!" But, after all, every means of communication is open to abuse, and has its drawbacks and dangers, if not investigated in the right spirit. Mr. Stead was well aware of this, and all applicants to the Bureau had this caution placed before them. Like all blessings, spirit-communion may become a curse, as a beneficent drug may easily become a poison, or as "wine that maketh glad the heart of man" may reduce him to depths of degradation.

Early in the beginning of his quest into the mysteries of the *Borderland*, Mr. Stead wrote:

> "Even if we can only make a single pin-hole in the curtain that hangs between the two worlds, that will at any rate show that there is light on the other side."

We may surely claim that in the two experiences I have just related, regarding prophetic messages, something larger than a pin-hole was made, and that for a few moments the curtain was drawn aside.

Curiously enough, we have been told that there is often as much scepticism among those who have left the earth-conditions, as there is with us on this side, regarding the possibility of intercommunication; and that as with us also, some spirits are more highly gifted and more powerful than others in breaking down the barriers.

18

A Golden Year

~

THE MORNING SITTING USUALLY LASTED about an hour, finishing with the Doxology. A chair was always left vacant for Julia, at the right hand of which sat Mr. Stead. He afterwards left for his editorial offices at Kingsway, there to immerse himself in the world's affairs—"damp down" as he phrased it, some strike agitation, or war scare, or rouse the flagging energies of workers in some drooping cause. He was at Mowbray House again in the afternoon, remaining there as a rule till evening.

Most of the letters received by Mr. Stead in regard to the Bureau were very pathetic in their burden of grief and desolation. There were few banalities. But there were many irrelevant applications, and it became necessary after a time to issue a notice stating that "Julia's Bureau was not established nor could it be used as an office of 'Inquire within about everything,' nor as a fortune-telling establishment, nor the office of a racing-tipster; nor as a detective agency, nor an office for the recovery of lost and stolen goods, nor for obtaining information about overdue ships or missing wills." We had sundry inquiries under all those heads, from various parts of the world. But the human longing for "the touch of a vanished hand" predominated.

Among others came a quaint but touching letter from India, from a parent who had lost an only child and was anxious to get into touch with the little one, to ask it to try to "reincarnate" at an early date! While

Mr. King psychometrized the application forms, in order to "sense" the psychic conditions of each, Julia, writing through Mr. Stead's hand and mine, decided on the merits of every case. Her decisions were written independently, Mr. Stead and I never seeing what each other wrote till next day when the completed forms were handed in to be compared.

Two or three weeks after the establishment of the Bureau, and while things were adjusting themselves for future work, Julia wrote through Mr. Stead's hand that he and I must be "told off in this double service as her secretaries," for, she declared, she "found not the least difficulty in passing from one to the other," and could convey her message through us both with the greatest ease. That she was as good as her word is proved from the fact that of all the six hundred and twelve applications dealt with in the course of the three years, only once did her decision, as recorded by both, entirely conflict. This was explained by Julia as due to one secretary's lack of passivity and too great haste in taking her decision.

Applicants thus "approved" were duly notified, receiving a form to fill in stating what they would consider evidence that they had been in touch with their friends. This form they were to seal and keep in their own possession till the conclusion of their respective cases, returning it then to the Bureau, to be filed in the Archives. As the Chief said, "What satisfies one person will not always satisfy another. The trouble with most people is that they never know when they are satisfied. Give them a test, they rejoice; then they wobble again and want more. St. Thomas was the pattern sceptic; he asked for a test, but having received it he believed."

The working of the Bureau was carefully explained in a small pamphlet, which was sent to every inquirer, though, judging by results, the latter often failed to read it. Frequently by return of post would come a most irritating list of questions, not one of which would have been necessary had the pamphlet been read. In particular, our Indian correspondents were as ingenious as incorrigible in this respect. As many as twenty and thirty questions would be asked concerning ancestors, going backward even to the "third and fourth generation."

As a rule the personal sittings gave best results. But the "psychometry" was often extremely good. The following is a typical example. Someone sent from India a little wooden penholder, which, he said, had been used by his son. Holding the pen, the sensitive, Mr. Robert King, who knew nothing of the case nor whence the pen had come, described a boy, giving definite details and apparent age. He obtained a short message from the spirit-child to his father, with whom he said the link was very close. The psychic added, "I feel Oriental conditions, and I hear a word like "Shanti" being repeated several times."

When the notes of the sitting were sent to India the father replied with much gratitude that he had no doubt he had been in touch with his son, a boy whose age and appearance had been accurately described. As for the word "Shanti" it signifies "Peace be with you," and was his child's greeting to him every morning.

A curious case was the following—a personal sitting at Mowbray House, with the psychic, Mr. Vout Peters. A lady came one day in much grief; she wished to get into touch with her husband. The sensitive, not knowing anything about the case, at once described a man's form standing near the lady. Mr. Peters gave a minute description of this man, and said he was with her always. She declared very decidedly that Mr. Peters must be wrong, the description was nothing like the person she wanted. Nevertheless he persisted he had described exactly what he saw and was certainly not at all responsible for the presence of the spirit. The lady was not pleased and the sitting terminated somewhat abruptly. She afterwards showed me her husband's portrait, saying, "You see that is nothing like the face he described." Nor was it. There the matter ended. But later I accidentally learnt through a friend of my own, who happened to know the lady in question, that she had been *married twice*. Apparently Mr. Peters had seen with her her first husband, clearly now an unwelcome intruder!

Where was "mind-reading "here?

When the Bureau was first inaugurated Mr. Stead said if one-tenth of the attempts were successful he would feel his experiment had been more than justified. But we found that each year the proportion of successful results was fairly evenly maintained at about one-third. Out of six hundred and twelve applications which were considered suitable to submit to Julia during the three years, only fifty-eight stated definitely that they had *not* been brought into touch with their friends. One hundred and fifty-two wrote that they were *uncertain* one way or the other. A good many cases were deferred, for various reasons; some were unfinished, and some had failed to return their reports. But one hundred and ninety-two, nearly *one-third* of the whole, wrote a declaration that they felt convinced they had been brought into communion with their friends on the other side.

The Borderland Library was not an integral part of the Bureau. No one was obliged to join it who did not wish to do so. It was a convenience provided for those who wished to study psychic literature. The subscription was a guinea a year, and Mr. Stead set no limit to the number of volumes borrowed at a time, nor on the length of time they were retained by the borrower! Membership of the library did not also include the use of the Bureau nor sittings with psychics. It gave no privileges whatever beyond access to the books and magazines. Nothing but Julia's own sanction made the Bureau available. It was, however, open to anyone who so desired to send a donation towards the expenses, exactly the same as in the case of a general hospital though this was left entirely to the free will of the applicant, nor would Julia allow any donation to be accepted until the case was complete. Very seldom was such donation offered. In by far the greater number of cases no offering was made at all. It is certain that this aspect of the matter never troubled our Chief. He never once asked me whether any sitter had made a gift. All he cared to know was that the object of the Bureau had been achieved. He was never too busy or too preoccupied to look up and listen with the keenest sympathy and satisfaction when one told him of some sorrowing person having departed with the knowledge that those they had mourned as lost were living still. To share "with another's need" his own joy, to spread the knowledge that death is no dividing abyss, but the gateway, if we will, to closer communion, was his dearest wish. He often said: "Of all my work, the Bureau is nearest my heart."

Various nationalities, creeds, and conditions, were represented by the applicants for Julia's good offices. The greater number were persons of education; doctors, lawyers, clergymen, and many men and women of eminence both in this and other lands.

A mournful interest attaches to the two last applications to the Bureau, received during the first part of April 1912, about the time Mr. Stead sailed in the *Titanic*. I sent the papers out to New York, immediately after him. But my letters and the forms were returned to me from America two or three weeks later. He had never seen them.

As to the monetary aspect of the Bureau, Mr. Stead told Julia in the first place that to maintain it adequately would require a thousand pounds a year. For the first year, however, it cost him considerably more. I quote the following memorandum of expenses from a letter he wrote me on October 6, 1909:

> "The cost of running the Bureau at present in salaries alone is £12 a
> week. Rent, rates, etc., come to nearly £10, extras about £3, making a

regular outgo, without regard to cost of furnishing, repairs, etc., of about £25 a week, towards which Julia's £20 a week is all we have. I ought to have another £500 at least.

Pray for it."

During the three years of its existence the Bureau gave upwards of thirteen hundred sittings,[33] every one of which was paid for by Mr. Stead out of his own pocket.

As has been said, the expenses of the Bureau far exceeded the £1,000 per annum estimated by Mr. Stead. Our friends on the other side assured us that further funds would come, but their assurances were made in general terms, and there was no attempt at a definite prophecy as before. Therefore in March 1910, Mr. Stead's lease of Mowbray House having expired, the Bureau ceased to work from there, and the Archives were removed to Cambridge House, from which the correspondence was then carried on. All sittings to applicants henceforward took place at the homes of the mediums themselves. Julia's Circle no longer met each day, but gathered every Wednesday evening at Cambridge House, Mr. Robert King being the sensitive as before. Two or three new members were gradually added to our number, but the proceedings were on the same lines as at Mowbray House. We greatly missed the daily sittings.

The Chief always hoped to re-establish them, and for some months he and I made a point of giving our hand to the Invisibles at 10 o'clock every morning, and exchanging results.

A letter which he wrote me on New Year's Eve, 1909, lies before me as I write. In it he urges me not to lose faith and courage, adding:

"Let us rather rejoice over God's lovingkindness and tender mercies which have so abundantly crowned this year with joy. If we could have foreseen all that we have received twelve months back, we should have said, No, it is impossible; it is much too good to be true. But it is true; all of it is true. Nothing can take away this golden year from our lives."

During that last year at Mowbray House Mr. Stead and I frequently left the office together in the evening, I walking with him as far as Westminster Abbey on my way to St. James' Park Station for Wimbledon, he being on his homeward way to Smith Square, carrying the familiar old brown leather brief-bag, tightly packed with letters

---

[33] Mrs. Wesley Adams and Mr. J. J. Vango were the two other psychics regularly employed by Mr. Stead for the Bureau.

and papers. I shall never forget those walks with him, along the Embankment, amidst the "lights o' London," nor our talks of a hundred things, past, present and future. He told me how in old days he used to pace up and down the Embankment with his dear friend Canon Liddon every Monday afternoon, when the latter was in residence, and how they threshed out "everything in the universe!"

Often, when Parliament was sitting, he would turn into the House of Commons in passing, to hear the result of some division, or debate, I awaiting him among the statues in the vestibule, as befitted a mere woman! I remember, much later, during the coal strike in March 1912, going to the House with him, and certain militant ladies having been much in evidence about that time, the constable on duty at the great stone steps insisted on inspecting the contents of my small handbag, to Mr. Stead's great amusement. When he rejoined me, some minutes afterwards, he remarked:

"I have just been talking to the greatest optimist and the greatest pessimist in the House." "Who may they be?" I asked.

"John Burns and T. P. O'Connor."

19

"The Voice Of Gladstone?"

~

I HAVE EXPLAINED THAT JULIA jealously guarded the privacy of the morning sitting. On rare occasions only she permitted the presence of a guest, but when she did so she generally directed that there should be a second séance, at which the stranger might be present; but this must follow the morning sitting. The one or two extra circles resulted in some curious developments. An eminent politician greatly desired to attend a meeting of Julia's Circle, and a special sitting was arranged for him. I was out of town at the time, so was not present on this particular occasion; but Mr. Stead wrote to me, enthusiastically describing various communications that came from departed statesmen, which struck him as so accurately echoing the sentiments of the said statesmen when on earth that he afterwards wrote an article embodying some of the messages, which was published in the *Fortnightly Review* under the title, "When the Door Opened." The country was on the eve of a general election, and it would seem that Mr. Stead formed a powerful focus for the forces then drawn earthward by sympathetic vibration, the first law of the psychic realm being that "like attracts like."

A famous political leader, still living, made some remark in a public speech to the effect that "It would be interesting to know what Mr. Gladstone thought of the Budget." The editor of the *Daily Chronicle*, in view of the developments indicated in Mr. Stead's article "When the Door Opened," then just published, challenged him to obtain the views of Mr. Gladstone on the political crisis, should the late leader be able or willing to give them.

The Chief as usual consulted Julia through his "automatic hand." She did not forbid the attempt, though she deprecated it. She said politics were not in her line, and the proposed interview must in no way be confounded with the object of her Bureau. The attempt must not be made at her morning sitting. But a special circle sitting might be arranged for the purpose.

Accordingly a small circle met and Mr. King transmitted a communication which, he said, seemed to come to him clairaudiently as though from a long distance. Mr. Stead considered it much like what Mr. Gladstone might have said had he been speaking through a long-distance telephone,—a telephone of very imperfect make and Mr. Gladstone himself unable to hear distinctly the voice of his questioner. Under such conditions the telephonic message would naturally be brief and fragmentary, and devoid of the ornate rhetorical style of Mr. Gladstone's public speeches. Mr. Stead was intimately acquainted with Mr. Gladstone's mode of thought, both by correspondence and interview, during the life of the Grand Old Man. But none of this seemed to be taken into account by the general public who learnt on Monday morning of the effort that had been made to "interview the august shade of the great Liberal statesman."

One point in relation to the "Gladstone interview" at Mowbray House has always remained in my mind. It was the one and only time that I ever knew Mr. Stead to read a prayer from a book as a prelude to a sitting instead of praying extempore. On that occasion he was, as he said, strongly impressed to choose the prayer of St. Basil the Great, from the Liturgy of the Greek Church.[34] It came to him as an impromptu mental suggestion, only a few minutes before the sitting began. I well remember his mentioning it to me at the moment. This very prayer of St. Basil was afterwards quoted by some of his critics as the most specially "blasphemous and sacrilegious" feature of the whole proceedings. Those who do not understand the truth of such "impressions" are not

---

[34] St. Basil, or Basilius, on account of his learning and piety surnamed the Great, was born at Caesarea, studied at Antioch and Constantinople, went to Athens, where he met Gregory Nazianzus, and returned to Cappadocia, where he taught rhetoric. Travelled in Syria, Libya, Egypt, visiting the monasteries. On the death of Eusebius, 370, was chosen Bishop of Caesarea. Refusing to embrace the doctrine of the Arians, he was persecuted by the Emperor Valens (A.D. 326-379).

to blame if they do not realize what, to the initiated, is perfectly natural, however mysterious, i.e., that minds still encased in the physical body may receive by vibration "thought-waves" from minds discarnate with whom they are in touch through mutual sympathy. Even so, asks the reader, but why the prayer of St. Basil in connection with Gladstone?

The following quotation from the pen of Miss Felicia Scatcherd throws an unsuspected light on this subject. Writing in the first number of the *Psychic Gazette*, June 1912, Miss Scatcherd, in her appreciation of W.T. Stead, said:—

"Mr. Stead invariably accorded to all the same welcome, the same sympathy, whether they hailed from the seen or unseen world. And this 'sweet reasonableness' constitutes him not only an invaluable pioneer of psychical research but the very prince of psychical pioneers, for he, more than any other investigator of my acquaintance in England, with the exception of Mr. F. W. H. Myers, laboured ceaselessly to discover the essential conditions which make certain phenomena possible.

"Lack of balance and judgment are the defects commonly urged against him, and not without some show of reason. Yet time and again events have proved him right, even when he was in a minority of one. But I will limit myself strictly to the sphere of his psychical activities, as the one in which I am best fitted to form an opinion, since for many years we were often daily in hot contention, only agreeing in our common determination to discover the truth of things. ... One prominent instance of this 'lack of judgment' is yet present to the public mind, when those of his own household of faith denounced most vehemently his brave avowal of what all professed to believe. I think it was an outsider who was among the first to expostulate against treating a man as an outcast because at the maximum of personal risk and self-sacrifice he attempted to demonstrate the belief of Christendom Man's survival of physical dissolution, and its Founder's assurance, 'greater things than these shall ye do.'

"I refer to the days of the 'Gladstone interview,' when many of his friends were against him. With less excuse than others I too was amongst the critics. He had handed me the latest attack, which betrayed the depths to which unregenerate humanity can sink when hounding down one whose horizon lies beyond its ken.

"Giving it back, sick at heart, I only said:

"'Why did you preface the interview with that Greek prayer? To you it can mean but little, and people are hurt by its incongruity.'

"He looked up with a pathetic expression of bewilderment.

"'My dear child, I had no thought of doing so none whatever! But when I came into the séance-room I was impressed to read that prayer. It was part of the proceedings. I could not suppress it, could I?'

"Some time later I was in Greece and spent a few days in the Ionian Islands, when I visited the home of the late Hon. Eustace Drakoules, the last Regent of Ithaca under the English. I was in the company of his son Dr. Platon Drakoules, recently member of the Greek Parliament. In the year of his birth Gladstone was his father's guest, and Dr. Drakoules, for my benefit, translated letters from the Lord High Commissioner of the Ionian Islands and others to the Regent of Ithaca, recommending Mr. Gladstone to his good offices and advising him to assemble some learned prelates of the Greek church, as his English visitor was deeply interested in all that pertained to the liturgy of Eastern Orthodoxy.

"I was especially fascinated by the Regent's letters on account of the light they shed on the life of that epoch. And it was some time before it dawned upon me that once again I had stumbled upon the justification of one of Mr. Stead's 'aberrations,' for assuredly the Gladstone of those days would have used the prayer Mr. Stead was impressed to read at the interview. ...

"Those who charge Mr. Stead with 'credulity'" concluded Miss Scatcherd, "overlook his possession of an 'automatic hand' that gave him *correct answers* to questions of practical moment year in, year out ..."

Nor must it be forgotten that Gladstone said of Psychical Research, when he accepted honorary membership of the Society, that it is "by far the most important work that is being done in the world," Whether or not we were actually in touch with the spirit of the great Liberal leader is not my point in thus going over old ground. Mr. Stead felt that he had been greatly misinterpreted, though he accepted it all with his usual philosophy.

"Do you not mind?" I asked him once, appalled at the shafts of malignity levelled at him, not only in certain sections of the press, but through the post in the shape of an avalanche of scurrilous letters and postcards, the modern equivalent of the mob for "this man hath a devil." "My child, if I had not been bomb-proof against that kind of thing I should not have survived the Maiden Tribute a week." I am reminded of his amusing "retort courteous" on another occasion, when he "turned the tables" on a certain popular periodical, which had attempted what it called an "exposure" of the Bureau.

In addition to gigantic letters on a hoarding several yards long near St. Clement Dane's, flaming posters met the public gaze the whole length of the Strand and Fleet Street. Mr. Stead promptly acquired a couple of these posters and had them placed in the windows of his office-entrance, "Review of Reviews," Kingsway, where the eyes of astonished callers were met by the announcement: "Stead and Julia Exposed!" No one enjoyed this more than the Chief himself. I think I can hear him now, exclaiming with a chuckle, "The Lord hath delivered them into our hands!" But the "Gladstone interview" touched another chord, and he certainly felt the refusal of the paper, which had in the first instance invited him to make the attempt, to publish the sequel, which is here given in his own words:

THE SEQUEL TO THE INTERVIEW ON THE BUDGET

Nothing that has been published in recent times has created so much hubbub as the attempt which I made three weeks ago to ascertain the views of the late Mr. Gladstone on the subject of the constitutional crisis which is now impending. The audacity of the attempt for a time took away the breath. But when the interview appeared, and it was recognized as bearing at least a strong internal resemblance to the recorded utterances of Mr. Gladstone on earth, the vials of wrath were opened and their contents discharged from press, pulpit, and platform upon my devoted head. I found myself gibbeted as the latter-day representative of the Witch of Endor, and was assailed in the same breath as the basest of political intriguers and the most unblushing of blasphemers. The *Daily Chronicle*, which invited me to make the attempt, flinched from the publication of the second communication, which was received by automatic handwriting by a friend of mine *who is neither a politician nor a professional medium*. It has therefore remained unpublished until now. But as the political crisis in England is now at its height, I think it may not be without interest to your readers to see what kind of a communication on the subject has been received, purporting to come from the august 'shade' of the great Liberal statesman.

When Mr. Gladstone was interviewed by a clairaudient he complained that he found great difficulty in getting his ideas through the brain of the medium, finding its mental furniture inadequate for the full expression of his thought. It was therefore arranged that he should write his ideas by the responsive hand of a lady automatist whose capacity for receiving messages in this way is phenomenal. The lady in question is not a politician, and she could not possibly have written the subjoined communications from anything within her own conscious brain. I wrote out some leading questions which I wished him to answer. She read them over aloud, and then sitting down, pen in hand, waited for the invisible intelligence to use it as her own. Of course I do not for a moment claim that there is any evidence whatever, other than the internal evidence of style and mode of thought, that the entity which moved her hand was Mr. Gladstone's disembodied spirit.

I only assert that we appealed to Mr. Gladstone, and that in response to that appeal the hand of the lady—*not a professional medium*, unversed in politics—was moved automatically by an unseen force so as to write the following political manifesto or declaration of principles. She did not know what she was writing while the message was coming; she was incapable of writing it herself, even if she had consciously devoted all her skill to its production.

The leading question that I asked Mr. Gladstone was, what course he would advise the Liberal Party to adopt if a collision arose between the Lords and the Commons over the Budget. After some characteristic prefatory observations the automatist's hand wrote as follows:

MY DEAR LADY,—We are on the Eve of All Saints' Day, and I am ill-attuned to approaching a long consideration of the questions to which you honour me by inviting my attention. I have not been following the course of political affairs since I placed my sword in its scabbard and withdrew from the dust and turmoil of ignoble party conflict.[35] It is with difficulty that I send my thoughts earthwards, and with still greater difficulty perhaps that you receive by vibrational responsiveness the impression I am desirous to convey. But I will endeavour to summarize my sentiments and to convey briefly what seems to me the only possible advice to offer the leaders of my party

---

[35] In Mr. Gladstone's Diary a passage occurs which curiously coincides with the phrase in the autoscript: "the dust and strife of ignoble party conflict." When Mr. Gladstone, at the age of seventy, made a tour of Mid-Lothian, on one of his great political campaigns, after a strenuous day beginning with a breakfast party in Glasgow and a rectorial address followed by a speech in the City Hall, and winding up with a Mass Meeting in the evening, the veteran leader made the following entry in his Diary: "Ah, what need have I of spiritual leisure to be out of the dust and heat and blast and strain, before I pass into the unseen world!"

upon the present crisis with which the country is now to all intents and purposes face to face.

As I view the situation in its conglomerate entirety—as I contemplate the Nation—the Empire (the latter, by the way, a synonym which I confess now jars greatly upon me by reason of the singularly blatant conceptions of aggressive domination which the popular mind attaches to the term), I notice that on the question of Finance, in all the multiplicity of its many-sided issues, the present crisis hangs. The final struggle, come when it will, will be fought out under whatever name may be attached to it—on the ultimate question of the right of the Nation as a whole to utilize to the uttermost its means of subsistence, and to dictate the terms by which every man contributing by his own exertions to the garnered storehouse of industrial wealth shall dictate the conditions under which he shall live. I cannot pierce through the mist which hides from me the intimate details of party programmes. I am not in full sympathy with absolute and unadulterated State control, which is only monopoly in another form, though to a certain extent a representative monopoly. I can only give you my broadest and widest opinion on the general principles at stake. When you ask me, "What is the chief point of concentration for Liberalism, and what is the chief danger against which you as a party should be on your guard?" I reply again that, as circumstances now stand, no matter under what subtle pretext an appeal to the country may be made, the striving and burning question is clear the battle when it is fought will be upon the one side an appeal for the primitive rights of man as man, and on the other by an appeal to the most sordid, the most self-interested, the most materialistic motives by which human nature in its baser aspects can be tempted and seduced.

Therefore, I would avoid as far as possible a sharp and sudden crisis which might precipitate an immature alternative that is to say, a development as yet immature in the present situation. Consequently, I adhere to my advice to the Lords to pass the Budget, because should they reject the measure they would thereby themselves precipitate the crisis which, I am of opinion, would be so hazardous at the present time. For the immediate result of a General Election fought to a finish on such grounds would be the unanimous combination of an immense majority of otherwise conflicting sections of the community, and an upheaval of a vast lava-bed of interrelated and burning questions at present smouldering beneath the surface, to an extent so revolutionary in its methods, so ill-prepared in its plan of campaign, that I shudder to contemplate the extent and depth and continuity of the probable catastrophe.

In such an alternative I, however, most certainly from my present outlook would counsel a definite and frank policy on the question of the Budget alone more particularly the land clauses—for therein I believe the real crux of the situation to lie. And in the event of our party being restored to office, my own action would have been, unhesitatingly and firmly, painful as in my heart of hearts I should have felt the extremity, to urge the creation of a sufficient number of life peerages to override the static element of determined and hostile opposition on the part of the House of Lords.

Furthermore, I should urge the realization of the Crown veto over that of the Peers, and should vest absolutely the control of fiscal matters in the hands of the Lower Chamber. I should deplore the necessity of a sudden elevation of the rank and file into the Chamber which, as I once alas! conceived it, should represent the flower, the dignity, the culture, and the trained and cultivated instincts of the finest types of British blood, bred for centuries to a sense of the responsibilities and obligations of their rank in the scale of civilization. I know too well that human nature cannot be always and altogether depended upon, and that this drastic policy carried to extremes might result in the substitution of a Frankenstein's Monster which would bring its own train of disabilities and undesired consequences. Yet it is an alternative I should without hesitation have counselled His Majesty to adopt were I impelled by force of revolutionary circumstances to deem it advisable.

In the event of an appeal to the country there is no point of attack so likely to be bitter and envenomed as the subtleties of those who have adopted Tariff Reform as their party cry, and no principle is so deeply involved and mistaken, no fallacy so widespread as that on which they base their appeal. Above all things urge the Liberal Party to sink minor differences and stand firmly together for their conflict with the hydra-headed monster of selfish privilege and inert obstruction under whatever name the people have been taught to do it homage.

In facing the constituencies my advice is to narrow your policy of attack into the smallest possible compass; concentration must be your watchword concentration upon the main points of agreement as you find them expressed in the terms of the Budget, and such overlapping incidental questions as naturally accrue therefrom viz., Old-Age Pensions and the Development Bill.

For the greater the extent to which you make it evident to the nation that it is a battle a hand-to-hand struggle between powerful class monopoly and the evolution of the human reason, between Privilege and Justice the more certainly do you strengthen your cause; for the Opposition will do its utmost to prevent the issue being fought out on those grounds.

But I am in confident hopes that the case will be pushed to no such extremities. What my judgment tells me is an inevitable course of procedure in the event of dissolution my rooted antipathy to forcing an extreme position holds in reserve.

Interests are so deeply interrelated; commercial enterprise, on which the future of this country tends more and more to depend, is so interwoven with the well-being of all classes of the community, that I trust most earnestly to the natural swing of the pendulum to restore equilibrium, when once the Budget, with some modifications of certain of its clauses in particular those relating to the licensing question has passed into law. If, however, you must inevitably fight, then stand firm as in the days of '76' and onward, and may God be with the issue! To enter more closely into the question of taxation and to detail my ideas regarding the reformation of the Second Chamber, I must regretfully and respectfully beg to postpone to another and more opportune occasion, I feel myself withdrawing from the condition in which I can hold communication with my friends who are still encompassed by the mists of earth, and I realize perhaps, if possible, more fully by force of the temporary contact the magnificence and splendid harmony, the profound serenity and lofty peace of the region in which I am now privileged to dwell. Yet I am not unmindful of the honour which has been accorded to me, nor I hope wanting in gratitude and appreciation, of the affectionate remembrance in which my name is held. I therefore subscribe myself your most obedient servant,

W. E. GLADSTONE.

Some uncertainty prevailing as to what Mr. Gladstone meant by his reference to the Royal Veto, he was asked to explain. He responded with the uttermost reluctance in the following letter on November 13th:

MY DEAR LADY,—I have already stated my opinions on the present political situation, in so far as I have understood it. From where I now contemplate the scene of action there appears to me to be no cessation of the elements of turbulence and discord, which, while they act as powerful incentives to a definite course of procedure, yet on the other hand tend to cloud and to obscure the ultimate question at issue, which is in reality, under whatever guise it may present itself the steady progress of humanity towards perfection an absolute condition to which neither individual nor nation has ever yet attained.

It seems to me that the time has naturally arrived when, in the event of the House of Lords rejecting a measure which has obtained the sanction and approval of an immense majority of those who are most distinctly affected by it, it seems to me that the time has naturally arrived when the remote and shadowy conception of some latent power—some hidden force—named Kingship, which has typified, and must ever typify, for the people of this nation something which draws from their united and collective individuality one of the most exalted sentiments which humanity is capable of feeling the sentiment of ardent and passionate loyalty to an Ideal must cease to be a vague nebulosity and must make manifest by decisive action that the Royal Insignia are less symbolic of the pinnacle of a vast and complicated social edifice than they are symbolical of the crowned and concrete expression of its own determination.

Question by automatic writer: "But would this not recreate an absolute monarchy?"

Answer: No, not at all. The idea I wish to convey is the abolition of despotism in any form, whether in the form of a Charles Stuart or of a body of unrepresentative opinion. A plutocracy is equally dangerous, and the problematical contingency of a Socialist monopoly will ultimately create its own solution.

But national development, like every other form of evolution, must follow its own natural laws, which as they are not, in their inmost essence, of man's making, are best to be seen and apprehended in their mysterious workings when the human spirit is in tune with its Highest Self.

Pray regard this as my final word, and believe me, my dear lady,—Your obedient servant,

W. E. GLADSTONE.

'These messages are almost exaggeratedly Gladstonian in form,' added Mr. Stead. 'some periphrases and involutions which were so long as to obscure his meaning have been removed. Otherwise the letters are printed as received. I guarantee the good faith of my friend, the automatic writer. She does not consciously write them herself. Whether Mr. Gladstone did or did not condescend to utter a word of guidance for the nation he loved so well is a question on which the reader will form his own opinions. For my part I see nothing improbable in such a condescension on his part, and if he did so condescend, the above seems to me very much the kind of advice he might be expected to give.'

Those whom Sir Oliver Lodge describes as 'good and earnest, though moderately intelligent religious people,' profess themselves to be immeasurably shocked by the suggestion that instead of spending eternity in 'dignified idleness,' Mr. Gladstone still feels a keen interest in the welfare of our country.

To all their outcries I reply by quoting Sir Oliver Lodge's question: Is it not legitimate to ask these good people whether, if an opportunity of service to brethren arises, an effort to seize it may not be made even by a saint?"

The original script is now in the Bureau Archives. Mr. Stead had it printed for private circulation, and it was shown, at the time, amongst others, to Dr. Platon Drakoules, scholar, poet, and writer, son of the late Regent of Ithaca. Dr. Drakoules said:

I think this the most remarkable utterance, entirely Gladstonian in sentiment, expression, style and import. If we exclude the hypothesis that it emanates from Gladstone we have only to conclude that it was written by a person expert in knowledge and entirely conversant with Gladstone's methods and thoughts. It is quite worthwhile to publish it, and it seems to me that it enhances his value as a man and as a thinker. It strikes me that if that had been spoken by him when living it would have gained for him an admiration which he did not very often attract. The conclusion that it comes from a Gladstonian mind is irresistible.

It was always Mr. Stead's intention, when the "psychological moment" arrived, to make known the true and complete story of his attempt to communicate with Gladstone. It never arrived during his earth-life, however, for the principal reason that his time became more and more engrossed with more immediately important things. A week or two after the "interview" the idea occurred to him to weave the circumstances into the form of a Christmas story, concerning which he wrote to me from Hayling Island as follows:

"November 20, 1909.
"Have got an idea and want you to help me to realize it. Why shouldn't
we write a story on the Crisis,[36] working in our spirit friends. The time
is short, but I somehow feel that a Christmas story of the Election
might achieve a great success."

He always followed up his fresh ideas with the impetuous zeal of a
boy, so I was not surprised next day to receive from him the opening
chapters of the story, with a demand for my honest opinion. He added
that he was under no delusion as to his merits as novel-writer so I
need not be afraid of hurting his feelings. Apropos, he was fond of
telling a story against himself concerning his first attempt at writing
a topical novel and the candid "cold-watering" it received at the hands
of his old friend George Meredith, to whom he submitted his maiden
effort *From the Old World to the New*. Meredith replied that some of
the characters were interesting and very well drawn, "but," he added,
"If any of your friends tell you that he likes the story as a story, *don't
believe him!*"

Mr. Stead's stories—he wrote several, including *The Splendid Paupers*,
and *Blastus, the King's Chamberlain*—were in fact sparkling political
dialogues strung together on the slenderest of plots, and I felt obliged
to agree with the author of *Diana of the Crossways*. I suggested that
those who read it as a story would skip the political dialogues, and those
who read it as a political manifesto would skip the story. Time being
then so short, he decided to drop the thread of the story and bring out
the political dialogue in the form of penny pamphlets, *Peers or People*,
Tracts for the Times.

A curious sequel to the "Gladstone episode," when it had long
receded into the background, came early in 1911. One morning when
speaking to me on the telephone Mr. Stead said: "I have heard from
Admiral Usborne Moore, who has come across a wonderful psychic,
a Mrs. Wriedt, in Detroit. At one of his sittings with her, Gladstone
purported to speak. The Admiral asked him whether he remembered
the name of the lady in England through whose hand he had given a
message. The voice then gave the correct name." As the story of the
"Gladstone autoscript" was only known privately to a few, we felt this
to be a very good test of identity, and Mr. Stead said that, subject to
Julia's approval, he would invite Mrs. Wriedt to pay a visit to England.

---

[36] General Election of January, 1910.

Let me here somewhat anticipate, by saying that Julia, on being appealed to, and writing as usual independently through both our hands, cordially approved Mr. Stead's suggestion, and Mrs. Wriedt, having been invited by him, duly arrived at Cambridge House in May, 1911, on a visit of several weeks' duration. Although the "direct voice" as one form of physical manifestation is well known in this country, yet the "direct voice" is as rare as it is wonderful. Mrs. Wriedt's visit was a marked feature in the history of Julia's Bureau. Many records of her séances both in England and in Scotland have already been made known, and it is therefore inopportune to enter into elaborate details concerning them in the present volume. It cannot be too often repeated, however, that the great number of sitters who have related their personal experiences were neither visionaries nor mystics giving utterance to the revelations of the "contemplative life," but practical men and women of the most widely differing types: professional men, clergymen, soldiers, sailors, society dames, literary men, scientists and others; and of these, many represented different nationalities, but all were in agreement on one fundamental point, namely, that they had held conversations with departed friends, who had spoken to them in the "direct voice," and of whose continued life and activity in the next state of consciousness they had received convincing proof.

Mrs. Wriedt's gift is not confined to the "direct voice" alone. In her presence the denizens of the unseen are occasionally able to reveal themselves as what are termed "etherealizations." These are intangible luminous forms, which glide about the room and pause before the various sitters, sometimes greeting them with a wave of the hand. Among the most beautiful of these were at times the forms of little children. These etherealizations are of course only visible in the darkness, but the voices can be heard perfectly well in broad daylight. Conversations in foreign languages, and in sundry dialects, frequently took place, and many of Mrs. Wriedt's sitters have on different occasions heard French, German, Danish, Norwegian, Servian, Italian, Spanish, Arabic, Hindustani, and even Croatian, uttered in the séance-room. Two and even three voices have often been heard speaking at one time to different persons. I have even heard as many as four and five speaking simultaneously, Mrs. Wriedt herself often joining in the conversation. Singing, also, was not uncommon; and sounds resembling the French horn, violin, and bugle, occasionally added diversified interest to manifestations always wonderful.

Of these things I do not speak without intimate personal knowledge. Nor can I but remember with gratitude that some of the most pathetic conversations I have had with my Chief, W.T. Stead, in the audible voice, since his passing-on, have been through the mediumship of Mrs. Etta Wriedt.

20

"Can Telepathy Explain All?"

~

"Having tried the hypothesis of telepathy from the living
for several years, and the 'spirit' hypothesis also, for several
years, I have no hesitation in affirming with the most absolute
assurance, that the 'spirit' hypothesis is justified by its fruits."

—DR. R. HODGSON.

IN JUNE 1910, MR. STEAD went to Ober-Ammergau and saw the Passion
Play for the third and last time. On his homeward journey he stayed
for a few days in Paris, seeing friends, and wrote me on June 10th, full
of enthusiasm concerning a great new scheme of "international import"
that was simmering in his head. He wonders whether he is destined to
"go in for international work on a great scale in the near future"; and
adds in regard to sign-posts: "There is no doubt that if I had the money
given to me I should feel it a call to leave you to run the Bureau, while I
went abroad one week every month," But that sign-post did not come.

The third seeing of the Passion Play had, he said, left him with
totally different impressions from his first. At the first, the sorrow of
the suffering Man Jesus came most powerfully before him. At the third
came only the sense of the joy of the world's Redeemer. He wrote of
it in the *Review of Reviews*, July, 1910, as "the Joy of being Crucified."

Joyousness was indeed the keynote of his life and his teaching. Despite his early Puritanism he had no sympathy with a joyless religion. "Granted that 'to please oneself' is the best definition of selfishness," he said, "the doctrine of loving one's neighbour as oneself transforms selfishness into a virtue! One might call it 'the Higher Selfishness': to love's one's neighbour so much as to make it positively preferable to please him rather than to please oneself!" A good example, this, of his quaint paradoxical reasoning.

But while his sympathy with real sorrow and affliction was absolutely boundless, he had scant pity for minor grievances. Gloom and pessimism were intolerable to his blithe and sunny nature. I remember his characteristic reply to someone's complaint that the weather was "dull": "All the more reason for letting God's light shine in our hearts and on our faces."

In the autumn of 1910, an article appeared in the *Contemporary Review* by a writer named Adolphe Smith, in which an allusion was made to the results of Julia's Bureau, ascribing the successful cases to "telepathy." Mr. Stead replied to the article by another, also published in the *Contemporary Review,* entitled "Can Telepathy Explain All?" in which he said that the value of articles like those of Mr. Adolphe Smith:

> "Lies in the fact that they frankly and fully admit the genuineness of phenomena which, the more closely they are examined, lead more irresistibly to one conclusion, which is not that of Mr. Adolphe Smith."

He illustrated his own conclusion by an "apologue" which so admirably condenses his final views on the whole subject that I quote from it the following passages: [37]

> "Imagine a village in the depths of the Sherwood Forest many years before the Roman Conquest of Britain. To the rustics comes one day a stranger who tells them curious things of an Imperial City in a far-off land of which they had never heard. He speaks of the wealth, the splendour, the luxury and the power of Ancient Rome. He tells of the roads of the Romans which stretch out to the ends of the earth, of their invincible legions, of their great triremes, of their science, their art, their literature. To the villagers he is as a man babbling in an unknown tongue of a people they had never heard of, inhabiting a country which

---

[37] *Contemporary Review.*

they do not believe to exist. In vain by the use of simple comparisons and homely metaphors does he try to explain to them what a legion is, how a palace is built, or how a galley is launched and propelled. His hearers understand none of these things. They know of no land but their forest and the surrounding country. The ocean they have never seen. Hence the most part of the stranger's talk is unintelligible, the fraction they can understand is incredible. Wearied with his attempts to make them understand, they refuse to listen and cover him with ridicule and abuse. ...

"So the years passed and other strangers arrived, making similar strange statements concerning the capital of the world. But as the stories of these travellers do not agree in all detail and as no one would undertake to show the villagers this alleged city of Rome, the rustics dwelt secure encompassed about in invincible ignorance, convinced that the Forest and the country round about was the world, and beside it there was none other. But as the years passed and the legions drew ever nearer and nearer the North of Gaul, rumours of their coming penetrated even the fastnesses of the English midlands, and the more intelligent of the rustics, recalling the travellers' tales which they had dismissed with scorn, began to admit that after all 'there might be something in it!' One or two of the bolder spirits even venture to inquire of the despised strangers how to find out if there were really any foundation for all 'that nonsense about the Imperial City in an unknown land.' Being directed to travel southward until they came to the sea, and then to cross over to the other side, they at first object on the ground that they have never had any proof there was such a thing as the Sea. Ultimately they think better of it and go. When they reach the seashore, they admit the fact that the sea exists, but they see no other side. The evidence that there is another side comes from the sea itself. The sailors who bring cargoes into port do not agree as to whence these cargoes come. Some say one thing, some say another. Some refuse to say anything, preferring to have it believed they brought their wares from the sea itself. Admittedly the boat-loads of fish were caught from the sea, and not less obviously many cargoes were shipped from English ports along the coast. Moreover, most of them can speak no English. Many are men of loose life and doubtful character whom no one would accept as credible witnesses upon any question, let alone one of momentous importance. And further, one and all are dependent for their livelihood upon the delivery of goods alleged to come from unknown lands. Of those who can talk there is a suspicious readiness to say what they think will be pleasing to their interlocutor, especially if they can thereby secure food or drink, or the wherewithal to buy the same.

"There is also reason to believe that the calling of navigators is fraught with much danger to life and limb. Many who have gone out have never returned. Those inquirers who against their better judgment adventured themselves for a brief season upon the waters of the sea are mysteriously subject to strange torments, which render clear thinking and close observation impossible, and threatened to turn the body inside out! All evidence proceeding from such a source must be regarded with grave suspicion. On the whole the rustic inquirers from Sherwood Forest, being shrewd folk and hard-headed withal, are inclined to report that there is nothing whatever to justify the story that there is any land beyond the Sea. If there be of which there is no evidence that will stand the test of critical examination it can only be reached by crossing the sea, a process which incapacitates the voyager for making accurate observations and which frequently costs his life. So the wise men of Sherwood return to their native forest, and pluming themselves upon their superior wisdom, to their inquiring neighbours they report on their return:

"We content ourselves with recording what we have seen and felt and touched. We can testify that there really is a sea. It actually exists; those who deny the possibilities of its existence were quite wrong. But there we stop. ... The proper thing to do is to investigate the sea and its sailors. There is nothing in all that they tell us to prove that there is any other land except that on which we stand. All that they bring into our ports they have obtained from the sea itself like the fish, or goods from other English towns. It is true that the sailors often deny this. But who would believe a sailor's yarn? No two of them agree. And you can get any tale you like for a glass of grog! ...

"This imaginary sketch of the insular and parochial mind when suddenly confronted with statements of facts which transcend the range of its own limited observation exactly follows the lines of thought with which we are so familiar in the voluminous writings of those who, after long denying the existence of psychic phenomena, are now busy explaining them away by referring them all to the sub-conscious self. What the sea was to the rustics from. Sherwood Forest in my apologue the subliminal consciousness is to Mr. Adolphe Smith and the school which he represents. They may now at all events be congratulated in having discovered the sea. ...

"What is useful is to quote their evidence as to the reality of the phenomena which it is still the fashion in some belated quarters to deny."

He quotes further from Mr. Smith's article, and from Mr. Podmore's posthumous work, *The Newer Spiritualism*, passages as to the genuineness of psychic phenomena and the momentous conclusions which on one hypothesis or another may be drawn from their occurrence, and proceeds:

"We of Julia's Bureau are each and all convinced by personal experiments, carried on for several years, that while telepathy and suggestion will account for many things, there is a large residue of phenomena which can only be accounted for on the hypothesis of spirit return."

As illustration he quotes a letter received at the Bureau in September 1910, in which the writer said:

"I must at least thank you for the privilege of a message through Julia's Bureau and tell you that though the message had no connection with the name and questions I wrote on the paper sent me to fill out, it was convincing of the identity of my departed husband and contained references to things known only to me and to him, and of so very personal and private a nature as not to interest anyone else."

Again, he quotes from the report of a Norwegian lady, Fru Ella Anker, who had sittings at the Bureau, and who wrote afterwards:

"I have at least got some results which my unconscious mind cannot explain, though it may be true that telepathy can explain nearly all things. I will first mention the case of George S. The sensitive described first his personal characteristics accurately as I knew him and then he said: 'This gentleman wants to show you something in his hand.' The sensitive then made a round ring in the palm of his hand. 'I do not know what it is,' he said, 'perhaps a crest.'

"I could not understand what he meant. I did not understand the word crest, but thought it was a signet. One of my friends who was present and knew George S. equally failed to understand it. But his wife, four months after, told me George had a round wound-mark in his hand caused by an explosion which forced a metal tube through the palm of his hand! I am convinced that this knowledge had never been in my mind or in that of my relative. I had only spoken with George S. twice or thrice and knew him very remotely, and neither I or my relation had been told anything about this. The medium's suggestion of a crest showed that he was equally ignorant."[38]

Having thus dealt with the theories of the subconscious self and telepathy, Mr. Stead's article concluded:

"There remains the convenient hypothesis dear to many good people, that these intelligences can communicate with us from beyond the grave, from the prophet Samuel down to the revenants of the present day, are one and all subtly devised personations of the Evil One. ... But as the sin against the Holy Ghost as we have recently been reminded was giving the Devil credit for achievements not his due, we shall do well to be chary of adopting this explanation of the messages described above. ...

"We are surrounded by a great cloud of witnesses whose forms some mortals can see, and whose voices are audible to many amongst us. ... If ... it be true, as all religions have ever taught, that we are compassed about by a great multitude which no man can number, of angels, ministering spirits, and the spirits of our beloved dead, amongst whom may also lurk malign intelligences, deceiving spirits, ministers of evil, the subject is one which calls still more imperiously upon the careful study of all serious men. For the door is now open. With the development of the Sixth Sense the denizens of that Other World are no longer invisible and inaudible to mortal man."

Apropos of telepathy and the foregoing, one or two small examples of Mr. Stead's own gift as a "transmitter" may be of interest. At home one afternoon and whilst reading an automatic message Mr. Stead had sent me a day or two previously, I suddenly felt conscious that he wished to ask me something. So strong was this impression that I at once went out to the nearest telephone. No sooner did he hear my voice, and before I could question him, than he exclaimed from the other end of the line: "Oh, I am so glad you rang up. I was just going to send you a telegram. I want you to post that X—— message so that it will reach me tonight. I want to send it out to J—— by this mail."

---

[38] The sensitive was Mr. J. J. Vango.

In this case he had not *consciously* telepathed, but was actually thinking hard at the moment of the very message I was reading. Curiously also, I had an appointment out of doors some half hour later, so it is just possible that had I not yielded to the impulse to telephone, his telegram might not have reached me in time for the message to be sent to him at once.

Another time, when he consciously "called" me, and I received the impression, it was apropos of a MS. he had sent me to read some time before.

"There was no immediate hurry," he said, so in the pressure of other work I did not immediately return it, but put it on one side to read at leisure. One morning suddenly I bethought me of the MS. and a conviction came that at some unexpected moment there would come a demand for its return. I at once finished reading it, then put the rather bulky parcel in a conspicuous place, intending to take it up to Mr. Stead next day. A little later the same morning I felt a moderately strong impression that my Chief wanted something, but the MS. had then left my mind. On ringing him up he said, "Have you a MS. there called——? A man was here about an hour ago asking about it, and I told him you had it."

He used to say one should never disregard those mental "calls," but always respond to them if possible, even at the risk of being mistaken. But I fear I did not cultivate the faculty, for it seemed to me then that it might be easy to set up an automatic "idea." But, for those who have sufficient leisure, it might be possible in time to train the mind to distinguish between the real "call" and the "false alarm." My own experience tends to show that the direct conscious effort to telepath is much less frequently successful than the so-called "involuntary" thought. As an instance of a message being intercepted by the wrong "receiver" I remember once feeling what I thought was a "call" from my Chief. On ringing him up he said that he had telepathed not to me, but to Miss Scatcherd. Miss Scatcherd is an extraordinarily good "receiver," but on that occasion I believe she did not receive the "call," which I, it would seem, had unconsciously deflected. When thus experimenting Mr. Stead often caused one of his secretaries at the office to make a note of the exact time, and the message, in order to check results.

While on the subject of telepathy, it is an interesting point, in regard to Julia's Bureau, that by careful testing, telepathy as an explanation of spirit-communion absolutely broke down. Julia had, in the beginning, directed that each applicant should be asked to fix his mind during the sitting on some name having nothing to do with the discarnate friend. Obviously, if telepathy were the explanation of successful results, it would take effect in such cases also. Of course this "telepathic test" could only be applied in the personal sittings. But not in one single instance did the sensitive receive from the sitter's mind the name which was being strongly projected for that very purpose.

After the Circle ceased to meet daily, the Chief for some time tried to keep up his own half-hour's conference with the Invisibles every morning in his Sanctum at Kingsway, while I sat, at the same time, 10 to 10.30, at Wimbledon. We exchanged by post each day the automatic messages thus received at what he called "our disunited Circle sittings." But it was difficult to keep this up with the unfailing regularity of the Morning Sittings at Mowbray House. He continued, from time to time, to receive curious little instances of the accuracy of his "automatic hand." For example, a manuscript of some importance had been sent to Mr. Stead which he passed on to me for perusal. I duly read and returned it to him, but in the pressure of business it is small wonder that he forgot the circumstance. He wrote me a few days later saying that the owner of the MS. wished for its immediate return, so would I "please hurry up and send it." I explained that I had already done so. Nevertheless the Chief was so certain that I was mistaken, that he dashed down to Cambridge House and made a hurricane-like upheaval of the archives, then departed, still with the lingering conviction that it must be there. Next day, 14 April, 1910, came a letter from him, saying:

> "John King wrote with my hand and said that the E—— Manuscript is in Kingsway. Miss Lawrence and I have looked all over the place and cannot find it."

Later followed the triumphant announcement:

> "Cheers for John King! Miss Lawrence has found the MS. after all, and it was just as John King said!"[39]

---

[39] Every spiritualist is familiar with John King, the "Great Control," who in earth-life was Sir Henry Morgan, Governor of Jamaica, during the latter part of the seventeenth century.

Our results were frequently interesting, in their confirmatory allusions to passing events.[40] A rather amusing example of a "Julia" message, of which the purport through both our hands was identical, was obtained when my Chief and I were some seventy or eighty miles apart, he at Hayling Island, I at Wimbledon.

It had reference to a curious item in the Bureau's history no less than an offer, by the management of a well-known Variety Theatre, to Mr. Stead, on his own terms, to appear nightly for a week with Julia's Circle on the stage of the Hippodrome! I think the management must have been somewhat surprised to receive a most decided refusal, for on Mr. Stead's sternly demanding, "Are you not aware that this is a religious service?" the answer was, "Quite so. We want the whole performance!" As usual the Chief suggested we should ask Julia's views—as we sought her opinion on most things. Our letters crossing in the post next day contained an answer identical to both. She emphasized Mr. Stead's refusal, but added a curious "rider" through both our hands. In sending me his script he wrote:

> "I think Julia is splendid. She had to buck-up so hard against your stained-glass, your prejudice against the idea, that she had no time to consider with you as she did with me why I could not go on the stage. The important thing is that she told both of us the one incredible thing, viz., that *per se she rather preferred the Hippodrome to the S.P.R. as a means of propaganda!*"

---

[40] For various reasons I do not quote these confirmatory manuscripts. They are all, however, in existence in the Archives. Their interest for the most part consists in their identity of purport. E. K. H.

21

The World-Man

~

"A great Heart, laid open to take in this great Universe and
man's life here, and utter a great word about it."

~ CARLYLE: *ON HEROES.*

ON THE 18TH MAY, 1911, Mr. Stead delivered an address to the
Union of London Spiritualists, which was destined to be his last
public utterance on other-world themes, and it is interesting
to compare his conclusions as expressed that day with what had been
his outlook eighteen years before, at the beginning of his quest.

He dwelt with special emphasis on two discoveries which he had
made since the beginning of Julia's Bureau. First of all, he said, he had
learnt that all human beings are "amphibious," because they dwell in
two elements. They live both in physical bodies and in the spiritual
world. "There is not a materialist on earth," he declared in his forceful
way, "who could live a week if he did not, in the course of that week,
enter the spirit-world by the simple process of going to sleep!" It is
then the Ego detaches itself from its prison-house of flesh and is able
to commune with those with whom it is in closest mental and spiritual
kinship, but from whom, in its waking moments, it is divided by the
barriers of the physical senses. He instanced the case of a lady, a friend

of his own, who habitually received communications from her son through a planchette. Often when writing messages the boy would say:

"Mother, I told you *that* last night,—but I forget, you do not remember those things when you return to your side!" The brain has not as a rule any recollection of what the soul has learnt in its wanderings through the etheric realms. But the soul gains strength and refreshment during its temporary freedom from the cramping limitations of the earthly body, and absorbs knowledge which filters sometimes through to the physical consciousness as what are called "intuitions," those subtle, mysterious promptings, echoes of spirit-memory which now and again come to us all. The fact of our living consciously partly in the physical and partly in the spiritual world, said Mr. Stead, had come to him as a relief, in view of the sense of sorrow and separation felt by our departed friends. If they were able to communicate with us when we slept, their sense of sorrow and separation could not be so keen as that of ourselves whose physical part had no memory of what passed in sleep. Another discovery that also came to him as a relief was this: two or three years before, he had thought that the friends on the other side were always longing to communicate with earth. He had learnt, however, that while those with whom we had bonds of love and sympathy wished to keep in touch with us, not only when we slept but at other times, the great majority did not care to do so. The chief anxiety of our friends was to assuage human grief by awaking in us the same sense of conscious communion as they themselves enjoyed. That was the only important point on which Julia had made any correction in the revision of her Letters. When she first wrote she thought everyone on her side was anxious to keep in touch with the world they had left. But she had gradually learnt that the intense desire for communication did not last. She wrote that after greater experience she had found that the number who wish for it is comparatively few. When emigrants arrive in a new country their hearts are in the old world. They long to hear from the old home. But after a time in most cases new interests arise and they gradually cease to correspond. So it is with those who pass to the Land of Light, where life is even more absorbing. Of this she wrote:

"When the family circle is complete, when those we love are with us, why should we wish to communicate? Our life lies on our own plane. But that is no reason why you should not use your best efforts to establish a Bureau. What my Bureau will do is to enable those who have newly lost their dear ones to have messages. The first important work of the Bureau is the evidence it will afford of the reality of this world. How immense, how multifarious, will be the result of the recognition of that reality. It will revivify and re-energize the whole of the religious and ethical systems of the world."

Though our Chief welcomed gladly, for the sake of others, any effort made by those on the other side to pierce the barrier, for himself he valued most those evidences of spirit-presence which, as he expressed it, "are apprehended by the inner senses of the soul."

"You hanker too much after the Voices. I regard them as useful only for convincing materialists," was his reply to a hope of mine that this fascinating form of manifestation might develop more generally among psychics today. What are known as "physical phenomena," had little personal interest for him. He admitted their great scientific value when attested by trustworthy and competent witnesses, but not as aids to the soul in its progress on the Mystic Way.

Mr. Stead's personal presence at the Bureau was much interrupted during the last twelve months of his earth life, for during the summer and autumn of 1911 he twice visited Turkey. The first time—in July— he went with the intention of studying the Balkan situation at close quarters, and in the hope of inspiring the young Turks to avail themselves of the then prospective Salonica Conference to justify their existence as the party of "Union and Progress." To his seer's vision the political horizon was already full of portent; ominous of cosmic cataclysm in the all-too-near future.

His brief halt in Paris was as usual taken up in seeing friends, and writing articles and letters far into the night. By his wish I forwarded to him daily every communication of psychic import, and his replies are almost in the nature of a diary, a quaint mixture of high politics and the *Borderland*, very interesting to read. Empress Catherine was as usual his chief source of inspiration as regards affairs of the Near East. "I wish," he wrote from the Hotel Bristol, Paris, on the 10th July, "I wish you would let Catherine write with your hand exactly what policy she wishes me to pursue in Constantinople. I will ask her to write also with my hand. ..."

During his stay in Constantinople he had an audience with the Sultan, at which the Court Chamberlain, Sir Loutfi Bey, who spoke English admirably, acted as interpreter. Mr. Stead, in his characteristic manner as of a prophet of old—"Thus saith the Lord!"—pressed urgently upon the attention both of His Majesty and the Grand Vizier "the absolute necessity of following a policy of peace and reform and avoiding any collision with the Balkan States."

He took counsel also with many important officials, eminent in Ottoman affairs, and everywhere and to everyone he strenuously advocated the Catherinesque policy of "Peace and Unity" as the watchword for present and future.

When he returned to London, early in August, well satisfied with his mission, having "delivered his message," the threatened strike of railwaymen which had been overhanging this country like a cloud had just been declared. He went at once to Liverpool to interview the leaders of the strike, and expressed his own views on the industrial outlook in an article which he called "The Nightmare of Civilization." In it he instanced H. G. Wells' gruesome story, *The Sea Raiders from the Depths*, as giving "a vivid and realistic picture of the helplessness of Society in the presence of those grim elemental forces" which are wakened and let loose from the deep by war. He also called attention to "the astrological forecast of trouble to come, indicated by the malefic conjunction of Saturn and Mars at 11.51 on Wednesday, August 15."[41]

"It is a great relief that the Strike is over," he wrote a few days later, when the storm-cloud had lifted. "But what a lesson, and what a memory!"

In September, Italy's sudden descent upon the Turkish vilayet Tripoli placed Turkey and Italy in a state of war. Mr. Stead hotly denounced the seizure of Tripoli as an act of "international brigandage" and championed with ardour the Ottoman cause, to the surprise of many of his friends and enemies who regarded him as a confirmed anti-Turk, not realizing he was *anti* only what was to him a breach of some common principle of humanity. When, as in the seventies, Turkey was the aggressor he wielded his pen against her. But now that Turkey was the subject of aggression by another Power he took up her cause. He

---

[41] Astrology was not of especial interest to Mr. Stead, but the Editor of the Occult Review quotes an occasion on which it received his warm championship, like many another unpopular subject. "When the astrologer, Penney, was convicted under the Vagrancy Act, the judge was reported as observing, in passing sentence, that it was absurd to suppose that any intelligent person could believe in such a superstition as Astrology. Stead was down upon him in the *Pall Mall Gazette* like a ton of bricks. 'seldom,' he said, 'has any judge uttered a sentence at once so arrogant and untrue,' and proceeded to prove that the bulk of Queen Victoria's subjects were at that very time firm believers in Astrology."

was never a mere party politician, but an eclectic, a statesman whose country is "that mystic kingdom of which the confines are Christendom itself," yet a passionate patriot who felt sometimes that the truest and most loyal service a man could render his country was to oppose her Government's policy when that policy seemed to him unworthy and unjust; he was an apostle pleading for the unity of mankind, "the Federation of the World."

In putting the case for Turkey he maintained that the Italian Government had broken one of the terms of the Hague Convention, to which she with other Powers had subscribed, i.e. the clause wherein it is agreed that "all international disputes should be laid by the disputants before a Court of Arbitration before proceeding to the ultimate extremity of war."

"Always arbitrate before you fight!" was the incisive phrase by which he sought to make that ideal a popular maxim.

In October some of the "Friends of Peace" held a private meeting at the house of Mr. J. E. Milholland, an American gentleman living at South Kensington, and Mr. Stead and another were nominated to proceed at once as delegates to Constantinople and Rome respectively "to remind the warring powers of their obligations and opportunities and to make a final appeal to each of them to refer the merits of the dispute to Arbitration."

Our Chief left London for Paris, again *en route* for Turkey, on Sunday, October 8. He gave a small luncheon party to a few friends the day before his departure, and I remember so well he was in one of his brightest moods, the mood of joyous serenity that lifted his spirit at times when he felt that, as he phrased it, the "Senior Partner" had entrusted him with some special bit of work, the success or failure of which was not his concern, "but the Father's," That thought was re-echoed in the characteristic farewell letter he sent me the evening before he left home.

On reaching Constantinople he had a second interview with the Sultan, and wrote me with delight that his glorious Peace Pilgrimage was at last to come off. The Turks had received with alacrity his suggestion that a band of Ottoman pilgrims should travel from Court to Court of Europe, appealing for Arbitration. The idea of the Turks appearing as Herald Angels before the European Concert attracted him irresistibly.

Later, when lunching with Miss Lilian Whiting, he jotted down for her use a few notes of that memorable interview at the Dolmabahce Palace, which he considered one of the best he had ever had. Through

Miss Whiting's kindness I am enabled to quote these notes exactly as set down by Mr. Stead. They contain the gist of the message he felt convinced he was sent by the Senior Partner to deliver to the Turk in his extremity.

W.T. S.: "How is your health, your Majesty?"

The Sultan replies: "My health is good, but my heart is broken."

I: "I know you are a religious man, and therefore know that Allah often sends his best gifts in disguise."

He: "Yes."

I: "Then you will not misunderstand me if I tell you I have come from London to congratulate your Majesty on the greatest blessing that has come to Turkey since you came to the throne."

He: "What is that?"

I: "The Italian attack upon Tripoli." He looked amazed.

I: "The Italian attack is highway robbery, a crime which words fail to describe. But it has been the greatest blessing to Turkey, and that I will prove."

He: "Can you indeed? Go on."

I: "What are the two greatest dangers that always threaten the Ottoman Empire? First, outside; second, inside. Outside danger, hatred, distrust of Turks. At one stroke the Italians have transformed this into sympathy. All your friends could not in twenty years have made so good a change in the outside atmosphere as Italy has in one week. Secondly, inside danger of fierce rancour between races, religion, and parties. Nothing unifies Empire like attack from without. Arabs fighting against you yesterday fighting for you today. So it will be with other races. More has been done for Ottoman unity by the Italians than you and all your friends could do."

He: "Yes, that is true, and it is good." ...

The Sultan: "Are you going with the deputation?"

I: "Yes, but I hope you understand that I don't want one piastre of the £1,000 you promised for the deputation."

He: "But you ought to have your expenses."

I: "No, I pay my own expenses."

He: "But that is wrong. Why not take your expenses?"

I: "Because my independence is worth more to me than my expenses."

He: "Then you must at least let me give you a little present."

I: "No, I cannot accept your present."

He: "I don't mean money."

I: "I did not think you did. I thought you meant an Order or Decoration of some kind, and I never accept orders."

He: "No, I only thought of a little keepsake as a souvenir of your visit."

I: "Well, your Majesty, as you are so very pressing, I will consent, on one condition."

He: "And what is that?"

I: "That you will allow me also to give your Majesty a keepsake as a souvenir of my visit."

He (laughing heartily): "Quite right. We exchange gifts, as friends. Now we meet on terms of perfect equality."

I: "Heaven forbid. Your Majesty is the Sovereign of a great Empire, and I am but a little journalist."

He: "No, Mr. Stead, it is you who are my superior. I only have to look after the affairs of one Empire. But you look after the affairs of all the Empires in the world". ...

The Sultan: "Well, Mr. Stead, I told you that the Italians had broken my heart, and it is true. But I have not been left without compensation, for they have sent you to Constantinople to give me consolation."

The Sultan's gift to Mr. Stead took the form of a beautiful gold cigarette-case, bearing an inscription in diamonds and rubies. The Oriental splendour of the Imperial palace by the deep blue waters of the Bosphorus, the ornate cup with its silver holder encrusted with jewels in which coffee was served to him on arrival, recall the gorgeous surroundings of a scene in the Arabian Nights. The prince of journalists gave His Majesty a fountainpen.

Mr. Stead was much amused by a little sketch made of himself at the time as "His Excellency Stead Pasha," wearing a red fez and brandishing a scroll bearing the words "Boycott of Italy," As his articles on the crisis which duly appeared in the Turkish press had to be translated into Turkish and then re-translated into French, a curious error resulted on one occasion.

He had written "these unfortunates must make a clean sweep of those international brigands," but the Turkish translator, evidently at a loss for an equivalent idiom, reproduced the phrase as "these unfortunates must *tuer* those international brigands." Mr. Stead rushed off in wild haste to the office of the *Jeune Turc,* only to find that he was too late to suppress his supposed incitement to assassination, which duly appeared in print next day.

He left Constantinople on the 27th October, having seen all arrangements made for the departure of a band of Ottoman Pilgrims representing all races and religions of the Turkish Empire.

On returning to London he called a public meeting at Whitfield's Tabernacle and reported upon his mission. The meeting was extremely enthusiastic. He was supported on the platform by the Right Hon. Syed Ameer All, and Shakour Pasha, a Christian Ottoman from Egypt; by Mr. Milholland, Mr. Cunningham Graham, Mr. Israel Zangwill and many others. A large number of letters from sympathizers were read, beginning with the Lord Mayor and ending with the Rev. J. Campbell Morgan. An interesting feature of the evening was a detachment of Boy Scouts who acted as stewards. The following weekend he went down to Hayling Island and hastily embodied his views on the whole situation in a pamphlet entitled, *Tripoli and the Treaties: a Plain Statement for the Man in the Street.*

But the Pilgrimage hung fire. Forgetting his counsel of "Unity" the Turks broke up into parties, and, without the inspiration of his presence, the fatalism of the Ottoman temperament re-asserted itself. Here in England Mr. Stead felt himself at a deadlock between the lethargy of the Turk on the one hand and on the other the ineptitude of the Peace Party—who "do nothing but talk," he declared with irritation—and the indifference of the Foreign Office with its traditional attitude of cold water towards everything unofficial. His mercurial spirits felt the chill, but as usual he watched and waited for sign-posts.

> "The worst of my being in such an overstrained condition," he wrote from Hayling Island, "is that I don't get any messages free from stained-glass. We are all in the same boat in this respect. We allow all our own miserable anxieties, disappointments, and I know not what, to dust up and obscure the windows of our soul."

But he was soon filled with renewed energy. A few tranquil days by the sea, with his writing and books, his communings with the Unseen, speedily restored him to his wonted vigour. He realized more and more this need for the soul's withdrawal into the silence. He was in the deepest sense a mystic, feeling in his heart that "through every star, through every grass-blade, and most through every Living Soul, the glory of a present God still beams," The latent poetry of his nature came out in his once asking me to bring him a few sprays of the red japonica which grew round the dining-room window at Cambridge House; for, he added: "I want to give it to my wife. Red japonica was in blossom the day I proposed to her, thirty-nine years ago."

The same window bears today a large pane of glass cracked and starred by the stones of the mob which howled round Cambridge House, then his home, on "Mafeking night," trampling down flowers, tearing up rose-bushes, smashing the glass of the vinery to atoms, in its "Jingo" fury. Mr. Stead was proud of that window-pane, and would never have it replaced.

He was proud too that his South African policy was ultimately vindicated and that he lived to see a South Africa united under the British flag.

As Cecil Rhodes made Mowbray House his Mecca in old days, so in after years did the Boer leaders, when in London, seek counsel and inspiration from the man who had risked life and prestige in proclaiming his Imperial gospel of equal justice.

When in London over the week-end his great delight was to gather about him as many people as the drawing-room at Westminster would hold. Needless to say, these receptions included guests of all nationalities and creeds. Tea was followed by a lively discussion on some topic of the day. Whatever the subject might be, and however widely opinion differed, a spirit of harmony seemed to emanate from him and to influence all present, though sometimes the debate waxed very hot, as when, in December, 1911, the Persian crisis was at its height and once again his attitude in regard to the latter dispute came as a surprise to his "Peace" friends. He defended Russia's claim for the dismissal of Mr. Schuster, the American Treasurer-General of Persia, arguing that the demand was one which should have proceeded from both Russia and England alike, for Russia's protest against the appointment of a British official in Northern Persia, the Russian sphere of influence, was exactly the same protest as England herself would have made had a Russian official been appointed in Southern Persia, the British sphere of influence. "There are no such enemies to the peace movement as the so-called 'peace people.' They have no sense of political perspective." He made that remark in 1911, to a representative of the *Christian Commonwealth*, who interviewed him with regard to a proposal for the reduction of armaments as a possible part of the Peace Programme. Mr. Stead roundly declared that there could never be any agreement about armaments *until* the principle of arbitration is established and people feel they have a court to which appeal may be made and they can get justice. "At present there is no such feeling," he said, "and any attempt to bring in armaments at all would be most mischievous. ... We must begin by recognizing, first, that armaments cannot be reduced at present; second, that the only hope of getting them reduced in future is in saying nothing about them now. ... I agree about the importance of the reduction of armaments. I have been on that particular warpath myself for twenty years, but I have attended two Hague Conferences, and I tell you that you can do absolutely nothing with armaments until you have established an authority that is recognized as just, as impartial, to which people can appeal."

22

"The Talisman From Poland"

~

I N ALL AGES MUCH HAS been written concerning what is called "Black Magic," and its possibility is fervently believed in by many serious and level-headed persons. What I have now to relate may possibly be thus explained by those who profess to understand this dark form of occultism. I personally am profoundly ignorant of the subject. Mr. Stead disregarded all such ideas, and Julia, writing through his hand, said:

"I know of no magic but Love and Prayer."

Curious indeed are the extraordinary series of uncanny, often fatal events, which are said to have followed in the wake of the famous "Priestess of Amen-Ra," whose mummy-case lid in the British Museum, bearing her likeness, has apparently been the cause of so much disaster.[42]

A curious sequence of untoward occurrences "coincidences," if you will followed the coming into Mr. Stead's possession of a crucifix, said to have at one time belonged to the Empress Catherine of Russia. It was understood to have disappeared mysteriously from Muscovy, during the lifetime of that august personage. It came into Mr. Stead's hands in December 1911, exactly four months before he sailed on the *Titanic*. The crucifix was made of ebony and silver and was about three inches long. At its foot was a skull and cross-bones in silver. Behind, at the intersection of the arms, was a silver rose. When first I saw it I

---

[42] See "The Priestess of Amen-Ra: A Study in Coincidences," by A. Goodrich Freer (Mrs. H. Spoer), Occult Review, January, 1913.

supposed that the former symbolized Christ's triumph over Death, and that the latter represented the Rose of Divine Love. Mr. Stead greatly prized this supposed relic of the Imperial Catherine, and for some time he carried it about in his coat pocket. He wrote one day telling me about it, making in his letter a little sketch of the cross. The following Wednesday he brought it down with him to Wimbledon to a meeting of the Circle. Mr. King immediately detected very unpleasant "astral conditions" in connection with the crucifix and strongly advised Mr. Stead not to continue to carry it about with him, as it would be specially inimical to him. But our Chief shrugged his shoulders and smiled. The crucifix was handed round the Circle for examination then placed on the table, where it remained during the rest of the sitting, the silver skull and cross-bones gleaming in the red light of the lamp overhead. I so well remember Mr. King's transmitting several messages received by him clairaudiently, mostly of a warning nature, declaring that "the astral fragments of the cross were strongly charged with black magic" and that its proximity would be exceedingly harmful to persons not "specially protected" against these elements. There was no suggestion that the Empress was in any way responsible for the malefic conditions connected with the crucifix. On the contrary, it was stated that it had been associated with the sacred days of her youth and innocence. It had become a focus for "the black forces" long after leaving Catherine's possession.

Mr. Stead remained sceptical, but in the space of a day or two he became the victim of depression and *malaise* as intense as it was unusual. This lasted over Christmas and increased in intensity. The distressing symptoms at once disappeared, however, when Mr. Skeels took away the crucifix to have it "demagnetized" 'by a friend who was deeply versed in magical rites. Mr. Stead's health and spirits returned so buoyantly that he laughingly admitted there "*might* be something in it!" though he added, "it sounds like nothing but the most fantastical nonsense."

News then reached us that another friend who had carried the crucifix about for a short time had a sudden and totally unexpected reversal of fortune. And Miss Scatcherd, who was then in Egypt, wrote saying that she felt some troubled condition surrounding the Circle. One or two other persons who came into contact with the cross became ill, but I personally felt no harmful effects whatever. The friend to whom Mr. Skeels took the crucifix to be "decharged" writes as follows:

"The cross had nothing evil attached to it when it left me, that is confirmed by two other independent investigators who knew nothing of what it was.

"The cross had belonged to an Illuminate either in East Germany or Russia Warsaw, I think. Then it had got into wrong hands and had been used in the Black Mass. But for many years it had been laid aside in indifferent hands."

Mr. King, however, was not quite satisfied that the malignant conditions had been wholly eliminated, and from time to time he transmitted messages to that effect.

I now quote the words of Dr. Dillon, Russian Special correspondent of the *Daily Telegraph*:

"Our last meeting took place on the 3rd of January. He (Mr. Stead), my secretary, and I, lunched together at the Holborn Restaurant. During lunch he told me a thrilling story of an apparition of Catherine the Great, and the sudden appearance of a talisman from Poland, which brought ill-luck to everyone who possessed it. 'I have it now,' he went on, 'and I am curious to see whether any mischief will befall me, and what form it will take. Is it not thrilling?' Before lunch was over it was a question of my keeping the talisman (which I never saw) for a time, to test its fatal potency. But I declined. That was the last I saw of W.T. Stead."

23

Notes By The Way

~

A S MAY BE IMAGINED, MR. Stead was frequently interviewed with special reference to his spiritualistic beliefs. He was always glad to explain that his knowledge of spirit-return had not caused him to forsake the faith of his fathers. To a minister of religion the Rev. Walter Wynn who asked him whether the Spiritualistic movement would have any practical results in the religious life of the world, Mr. Stead said:

"Why—immense results. The rehabilitation of Christianity will result from a clear perception of the occult forces now ignored. Take the ordinary Church member: he not only talks as if he did not believe in another world but resents any proof of it."

"But does not spiritualism disown or deny the doctrine of the Atonement?" asked Mr. Wynn.

"I do not think so; and the best spirits who communicate with us do not say so. All my researches in spiritualism strengthen my faith in the essential doctrines of Christianity. My son is a firmer believer in them than ever. And let me say another thing: I get to see deeper occult meanings in many of the doctrines of the Roman Church. After watching certain materializations I am not prepared to deny the possibility of transubstantiation. ... The Mass possesses an occult significance. I have no desire to join the Roman Church, but I have lived to see a deep meaning in much of its teaching for instance, prayers for the dead."

"Mr. Stead was called to the telephone," says Mr. Wynn, in relating the interview,[43] "at which he informed some invisible person that another ought to be shot, and after verbally despatching the delinquent in this humorous manner, he appropriately supported the doctrine of prayers for the "dead," with a further defence of them," "Well now, Mr. Stead, I want to ask you whether, looking back upon life, you believe in Christ, a personal God, and particular providence?"

"Yes; Christ said I was to believe in Him because I believe in God, but I answer Him: I believe in You and therefore in God. *Christ is at the summit of spiritual perception.* He knew most about the spiritual universe. I accept Him as a revealer of the Father—a Person. Of course, when we try to form a conception of an infinite personality where are we? What faculty have we for the task? This I believe: there is a spark of God in every man. ... Every enemy you have is a man in whom Christ is imprisoned. Your task is to liberate the Christ in him. Then he will love and understand you. Be a Christ. It is a great message."

To the same questioner's inquiry whether he thought the departed ones can see us, Mr. Stead replied:

"Ah! the question rather is: how *much* do they see of us? Strange as it may seem to you they see earthly things through our eyes. But are we not all human telephones? Are we not nearly always speaking to each other without sight of each other?"

Telephone interludes, such as the "aside" described by Mr. Wynn, were frequent and characteristic. The loftiest Olympian flights were often interrupted by the telephone-bell, when the Chief would break off his discourse:—"Yes, I am Stead—W.T. Stead. ... What? *Ha!!* It is *you*, you, you old scoundrel! ... You good-for-nothing old ruffian. Why, I have been wanting to see you for ages! ... Come round and lunch with me at one o'clock. I am delighted to hear your voice again!" Then, hanging up the receiver, he would soar once more into the heights, as though such mundane things as telephones had no existence. He had an inspiring voice; a voice to infuse fresh hope into a beleaguered city in the midst of despair.

Several pictures stand out in my memories of 1911. One is of an April afternoon at the Crystal Palace, when the Festival of Empire was in preparation. Mr. Stead, whose interest in the Festival took him frequently to the Crystal Palace, found time to write of it in a delightful *Book for the Bairns*. I, having to see some rehearsals of the Pageant, for necessary

---

[43] *United Free Church Magazine.*

notes, was with him one day. We had tea on the Club Terrace, being joined, amongst others, by Mr. G. R. Sims, and I recall the sparkling psychic talk that followed, between the Chief and "Dagonet."[44]

Another memory-picture again shows him at Sydenham Hill at a reception to Colonials visiting England for the Coronation festivities. Mr. Stead, vigorously ringing a bell, gathered the large company together under a tree, in a kind of "druidic circle" round him in the garden of the Dominion Club once Sir Joseph Paxton's house and started an amusing discussion on: "Are the English Cold?" by referring inadvertently to his guests from the other side of the world as: "Our friends from the other world," at which everyone smiled, including the Chief himself when his words suddenly dawned upon him.

Then there was our "Christmas lunch," two days before his last earthly Christmas—which he spent in the North,—he loved those anniversaries and insisted on ordering turkey and plum pudding and all kinds of seasonable things—"to make it feel Christmassy," he said. In his sanctum later, in the intervals of dictating to two busy private secretaries he asked me for the names of any persons who would care to have his Christmas greeting card, a portrait of himself the last one ever taken in "prison clothes," on the last anniversary of the day. In my mind's eye I can see now the grey head bending over the table, as he wrote an inscription on every card. He wrote very rapidly, when taking automatic messages especially, and of his several fountain-pens his favourite was the one with which he had signed the first and second Hague Conventions, and "hoped to sign the third."

---

[44] Soon after the loss of the *Titanic*, "Dagonet "wrote: "I did not know that William Stead was on the *Titanic*, or that he had gone to America. The night before the news of the disaster came I had arranged to invite him to come and see this year's Cup Final with me. Then it became 'coincidence' all along the line. The first time I met William Stead to talk to him we were together with the Right Hon. Alexander Carlisle on a White Star Liner. When I heard of him for the last time he was on a White Star Liner designed by Mr. Carlisle. While I was looking at his portrait in the *Daily Graphic* a maid came in and handed me a rolled parcel. I opened it. It contained the April number of the *Review of Reviews* edited by W.T. Stead.

"He was the sublime crusader, earnest, eager, energetic to the end. He lived every hour of his life, filled with the zest of it and enthusiasm for its work. He died where he always strove to be—I say it with all reverence and affection— in the limelight. Whether his radiant spirit elect to be silent evermore or to seek communion with those on earth, God bless it in the *Borderland*."

24

"Traveller, Must You Go?"

~

"I have got my leave. Bid me farewell, my brothers! ...
A summons has come, and I am ready for my journey."

~ TAGORE (*GITANJALI*).

I CAN BUT DRAW TOGETHER now these stray threads of my recollections.

Mr. Stead's last article on the problems of the soul was written specially for the New Year's number of *La Revue Spirite*[45] where it appeared in January, 1912. In that article he dealt exclusively with his favourite theory of the "Multiple Personality"—for evidence of which he, like the late F. W. H. Myers, was constantly on the look-out. He discussed the problematical expression of man's personality under three separate aspects, each entirely distinct from the other, but having the same characteristics, and always acting in conformity to the mentality of the one Ego, or "hub of the wheel." He likened the physical consciousness to the concierge of a building, who is only imperfectly acquainted with the occupants. He instanced one case among several which had come under his own observation, and which claimed to be a multiplication of the same personality; "but," he added, "there are so many mysteries which

---

[45] Founded by Allan Kardec.

can only be cleared by patient and uninterrupted study, that it would be absurd at present to dogmatize upon information yet so vague and of which the facts are not accurately recorded." In conclusion he said:

> "I simply put forward views in accordance with my own observations.
> ... I am disposed to modify my way of thinking without hesitation
> if facts are brought forward which contradict my own hypotheses."

Thus, without prejudice, he wrote his last on a theme that had for him a constant fascination.

Spirit-return he considered a fact proven beyond controversy. But to the abiding and elusive mystery of "the ghost that dwells in each of us" he still eagerly sought the key. ...

How clearly do I remember, one March morning, in 1912, Mr. Stead's putting into my hand, in the sanctum at Kingsway, a cablegram which had just come from America, asking him to speak at Carnegie Hall, New York, on April 21, on the subject of the World's Peace. How little either of us realized at that moment that his "call" to the higher life had in such wise come.

The meeting in New York was organized by the promoters of the "Men and Religion Forward Movement," a movement which had for some time been in progress in the United States, its object being "to bring business methods into religion and to work for the attainment of moral ends with the same energy, concentration, and common sense that are used in the making of a great fortune," The meeting in New York was to be addressed amongst others by President Taft. Mr. Stead, writing in the last number of the *Review of Reviews* he was destined to edit, denned the movement as "an attempt to organize on a national scale the ideals of our old Civic Church," But, he added: "I am surprised to find an almost entire absence of any allusion, direct or indirect, to the fact of existence after death," He intended to call attention, in his speech, to that strange omission from the programme of a movement avowedly religious.

He did not immediately decide to accept the invitation, but said, as usual, that he would be guided by his "sign-posts," From many points of view it seemed good that he should take the journey; he was feeling the strain of overwork and the burden of many cares, and he hoped, and we hoped, that a few days on the sea which he loved, would restore him to his usual state of vigorous "fitness,"

Also an outcome far vaster and higher than the ostensible object, was declared by the "Other Side" to hang on this proposed journey to the Western world, which was "but the pivot on which the real issue turned." In his heart our Chief felt, and said, that he knew "some greater mission lay ahead."

We have often been asked did "Julia, "did none of our unseen friends, give "warning" in this case? Did Mr. Stead himself receive no personal intimation that an event was near which would bring all his earthly activities to an abrupt and sudden close? The question is a natural one. I can truly say that on looking over our records for a few months previous to 15th April, it is easy to find much that, read now in the clearer light of all that has happened, points all too plainly to some momentous change about to take place. But these messages were not given as warnings, rather as forecasts of some inevitable event, some great reinforcement of spiritual energy, something that would draw the worlds visible and invisible even closer together than before.

Among innumerable jottings I find the notes of an impromptu sitting, at which the psychic, a lady, said to Mr. Stead, in my presence, "You are going to have a gain and a loss. ... You will see the spirit people you have loved, in the darkness."

But we only took this to mean that the psychic foresaw a development of clairvoyance on the part of our Chief, a by no means welcome prognostication, for, writing me in regard to such a possibility, he said:

> "Clairvoyance is a precious gift. But I ought not to add this to my already driven-beyond-my-efficient-capacity mind and strength."

In March the psychic spoke those words. Less than a month later our Chief had passed through "the darkness" and had seen the faces of "spirit people he loved."[46]

His letters of the last three or four months are full of the usual characteristic sidelights, showing that along with the unconscious foreshadowing was still the buoyant interest in everyday affairs. The psychic undercurrent ran as ever beneath all things. I find the following reference to Empress Catherine, in a note dated 14th January, 1914:—

---

[46] A curious prophecy was made to Mr. Stead at a meeting of 'sJulia's private circle in May, 1911. Mrs. Wriedt being present we had the "Voices," and the spirit of an American-Indian, greeting Mr. Stead, called out mournfully: "Chief Steady! You cross big pond one time more, before you shuttee eye!" Admiral Moore, who was present, mentions this in *Glimpses of the Next State of Consciousness*.

"Catherine wrote, the other day, that I must go to Vienna soon. Curiously enough the Vienna *Neue Freie Presse* now telegraphs me to write them an article on Rosebery's alarmist speech."

His correspondence about that time contains many references to the probability of his revisiting Russia in the spring. He had almost made up his mind to do so, though each time he made preparations for starting something occurred to prevent it. Not to Russia was the journey that lay in store.

"Let us realize that whatever happens is really God's best, which is much better than our own," he wrote concerning one of those frustrated plans.

In February, for no particular reason that he could assign, he began to go over all his papers, gathering together and scanning documents which he had not looked at for years. Sending them down to me to put into order, he wrote on 4th February:

"I have been sorting up Julia's old letters. They are voluminous. I enclose you what she said about them. Some of the old psychic things are most interesting. Madame de Thèbes, for instance, in 1900, was wonderfully correct."

He wished for an opinion from Catherine on some question of ethics then under discussion, and wrote in answer to a script I sent him:

"I return you Catherine's beautiful letter. I asked her tonight if she wrote it. She said Yes, and that she read it through my eyes as I read it. She says you are a lute from which her fingers draw sweeter music than she could make herself. ... "

In February he gave a dinner to the staff of the *Review of Reviews*, and afterwards told them the story of Julia from the beginning, touching on various experiences and his reasons for having founded the Bureau. In speaking to me of this later he said: "It suddenly came over me that I ought to talk to them about it. Some of the men probably never were told before that Julia was a real entity, not someone I had 'invented.' I may never have another opportunity of explaining it all to them."

On April 2, I lunched with him for the last time, and we discussed the forthcoming anniversary—the third—of the opening of Julia's Bureau, April 24.

He said:

> "I am sorry I shall be away for the Bureau's third birthday, but I shall
> be with you in spirit. And we must have a special 'birthday party' for
> Julia when I come home."

Next day he came to the last sitting with the Circle at which he was
ever to be present. It was a beautiful afternoon, "full of the promise of
Spring," as the opening day had been, and he stood for some time on
the balcony leading from the library; he leant on the rail and looked
long and lovingly over the old garden for the last time, in the April
sunshine. A strange note of farewell runs through my memory of
that last evening. Julia's message to her Circle spoke of the pain of
forthcoming separation, and urged us to meet regularly "in all faith
and confidence" till the "joy of reunion." She chose for the hymn "Our
Blest Redeemer," with its prevailing burden of earthly parting. No such
hint of "pain of separation" had preceded his several weeks' absence
in Constantinople the previous year. He only intended to be absent
some three weeks from London, and his goings and comings were too
frequent to excite much comment, though we never failed to miss his
presence exceedingly. A sudden flight to one or another of the European
capitals, as international exigencies demanded, was the most natural
occurrence in the world. Yet never before had there been that constant
sense of "goodbye" that runs through all he said and did in those last
weeks. All who were in touch with him have felt the same.

For his reading that night he chose the seventeenth chapter of St.
John. … How vividly I recall the stillness of the room as he read; the
fragrance of white lilies and incense around us; and the vague sense of
foreboding that stole over me as I listened to the solemn earnestness of
his voice, dwelling on the words: "I have finished the work that Thou
gavest me to do." …

They were the last words he was ever to read in the room so dear to
us all as "Julia's Sanctuary." An eerie sense of something too indefinable
to call "presentiment" swept across my mind; perhaps a thought that
some day, however far distant, would come the time for our grand old
warrior to lay down his armour, having "finished his work," But there
was no hint that the great ship in which he meant to voyage across the
Atlantic was doomed.

He went to Hayling Island as usual for Easter, and from his cottage,
Holly Bush, the day after Good Friday, wrote:

"Good Saturday, April 6, 1912.
"Your note of Thursday only reached me this morning. ... O—— (you
know whom I mean) says this American trip will be a preparation for
the summons which will be authoritative, unmistakable, and decisive.
... The sun is bright here and I am very busy. ... Remember my address
in New York. ..."

Then followed these bodeful words:

*"I feel as if something was going to happen somewhere, or somehow. And
that it will be for good. ..."*

He gave some directions as to the arrangement of his psychic archives,
the records of years, which he said he hoped to revise and publish,
adding, as though in answer to some sudden afterthought: "But that
will be as the Senior Partner sees it is best."

He gave no further details as to the message from O——, but, almost
as though its purport still lingered in his mind, he closed his letter with
words full of subtle foreknowledge:

"You might ask Hilarion tomorrow whether he has any knowledge of
the Summons which says is coming to me over there."

By Hilarion we understood a highly-evolved Intelligence, one of the
spiritually great ones, on whom we did not often intrude our mundane
affairs. But Hilarion, writing next day through my hand, only discoursed
oracularly on human destiny, and hinted at the greatness of some
coming mission, vaster than any which had gone before.

May not the very silence imply that—however difficult to realize
from our earthly point of view—the time of our passing is known
and fixed in the "great scheme" of existence; that for our Chief his
time had .come; and that therefore no fiat was issued *against* his
being one of the passengers in a ship which met its tragic end by the
ordinary law of "cause and effect." ... That all unknowing though
the physical consciousness was that the earthly end was near, yet
some deeper spiritual insight divined it. Was it not as though his
soul were saying:

"I have got my leave. Bid me farewell, my brothers! I bow to you all
and take my departure. Here I give back the keys of my doors. I give

up all claim to my house. ... A summons has come, and I am ready for my journey."[47]

The day before he sailed he came up from Hayling Island and spent a long busy day, bidding many "goodbyes" and making his final arrangements, giving me instructions regarding sundry "pensioners "on his bounty, about whom he was anxious, and otherwise thinking and planning for all. He took some books, I remember, among them being *Letters from Julia* and a copy of *Plato's Republic*, to read on the voyage. A French translation of his book, *"Here am I; Send me!"* had just arrived.

"Me Voici, Mâitre, Envoie-Moi!"—He gave me a copy, writing my name on the title-page.

Next day he sailed. All the last touching details have been told. ... In the evening I had a little note from him, written just before he left London in the morning:

> "Just a line to wish you goodbye, and ... to wish you all the good things the Master in His Love can send you. ... "

From the *Titanic* he sent a card to my mother—a picture of the death-ship, posted at Cherbourg—writing: "Just a card from the ship to bid you goodbye, and to thank you for all the care and vigilance that you have shown as guardian of Julia's Sanctum."[48]

Several of his friends mention having received from him similar greetings of farewell, couched in terms of unusual intensity, such as he had not before sent on his departure abroad, even on much longer journeys than he had intended this journey to America to be. Yet through it all he was, as he said, "in famous spirits," and full of almost boyish pleasure in being on board "the biggest ship in the world."

From Cherbourg he sent me a letter, dated 10th April, 1914, describing the ship and his delightful cabin, and concluding with the words:

> "What Hilarion says is no doubt true of all of us. We are all children of Destiny, guarded and guided by angel ministers, and each of us is only allowed enough light and sensation to be guided aright. ...
>
> "Now, cheer up and be a rejoicing minister of grace and joy to all. ... Goodbye, for a little season, and rest under the Shadow of His Wings."

---

[47] "Gitanjali."

[48] Mrs. Harper's "guardianship," was entirely honorary.

Next day I had a second letter from him, full of sunny plans and anticipations, dated "Off Queenstown, Thursday, April 11, 1912." Still, to my mind, that note of curious portent lingered in the first few lines, in his hopeful wonderings as to what new work Destiny had in store for him.

> "The ship is as firm as a rock," he added, "and the sea is like a mill-pond. If it lasts I shall be able to work better here than at home, for there are no telephones to worry me, and no callers. ... "

Then followed numerous directions regarding various things he wished to find ready on his return; a few words of hope for the future, and, for the present, Farewell. ...

Thus our Chief left us, for "The Other World—Across the Sea."

A Voyager

25

"The Promised Land"

~

"Still, still my song shall be,
Nearer, my God, to Thee:
Nearer to Thee!"

I T WILL BE REMEMBERED THAT when the news of the disaster to the
Titanic was first flashed across the wires, anguishing in its brevity,
it was followed a few hours later by reassuring telegrams stating
that the "*Virginian* was standing alongside the *Titanic*, and there was
no danger of loss of life." Even when next day that false sense of security
was taken away, and all who, because of it, had lived for a few hours in
a fool's paradise, were forced to realize the full horror of the disaster
as one detail more heartrending than another filled the columns of the
press, yet we could not, would not, believe that our Chief was amongst
those who were spoken of as "lost." It was utterly impossible to realize
that he, the tower of strength, he so full of "the joy of living," had been
thus suddenly snatched from the work and the world he loved. Though
well we understood he would not be among the fraction of survivors
the *Carpathian* was taking to New York, yet we clung to the hope that
he had been, as someone phrased it, "saved in spite of himself." That
perchance some other vessel had found his half-conscious body among
the wreckage—to any and every theory, no matter how wild, we held
with the tenacity of despair, blind to aught but the supreme conviction

that at any moment might come a cable, bringing the "welcome word of good cheer," the joyful assurance that he was safe. Safe indeed he was, but not in the way selfish human nature demands. ... One pictured his trying with all his might to send telepathic messages to one and another of his friends. If overstrung imagination and intense desire were the solution of clairvoyant vision, as the unknowing suggest, how often would we not have seen him! I refer to these details now, merely to give the reader some idea of a state of mind which would almost completely block psychic intercommunication, according to all known laws and experience. When during the afternoon of Wednesday, two days after the disaster, my mother told me she had clairvoyantly seen Mr. Stead, and that she feared the worst, as he looked so white and dazed, his face anxious, his eyes dim, we still refused to attach any serious meaning to her vision, and the strain and suspense of alternate hope and fear continued for days, till one could hope no more.

Few and meagre were the details of his last earthly moments when at length they came, yet they tell us what we would expect to hear. While waiting at the office of the White Star Line for authentic news of survivors, I had seen on a list the name of Mrs. Juanita Shelley, an American lady who, but a week or two earlier, had called at the office to make some inquiries regarding the Bureau. I wrote at once to an address I thought might possibly find her, and after some weeks had the following reply from her husband:

"MONTANA, U.S.A.,
"May 7, 1912.

"MY DEAR MISS HARPER,—
"Your letter of the 23rd to my dear wife received this morning. As she is still too weak to answer in person, I am acting as her secretary.

"Although Juanita was not personally acquainted with Mr. Stead she knew him well by sight. He behaved as all those who know him would have expected, a true man to the end. During the last minutes on board, my wife saw him assisting women and children to make their escape, and afterwards during those awful moments when the ship was sinking she could still see him upon deck awaiting the last call. .

"The average person of today will never understand the wonderful effect the music from that brave little orchestra had upon the souls passing into another state. Their memory on this planet will ever

188

be kept green.[49] The vibrations of that sweet old hymn, 'Nearer, my God, to Thee,' eased many a path during that transition from earth to spirit life, as you, Miss Harper, will be able to appreciate, student of the occult as you are.

"How the whole world mourns the loss of your noble chief, a real man!"

Some time afterwards I received a letter from Mrs. Shelley herself:

MY DEAR MISS HARPER,—
"Your letter received and I hasten to grant your request. I was only on deck a short time, until mother and I took to the lifeboat.

Your beloved Chief, together with Mr. and Mrs. Strauss, attracted attention even in that awful hour, on account of their superhuman composure and divine work. When we, the last lifeboat left, and they could do no more, he stood alone, at the edge of the deck, near the stern, in silence and what seemed to me a prayerful attitude, or one of profound meditation. You ask if he wore a life-belt. Alas! no, they were too scarce.

My last glimpse of the *Titanic* showed him standing in the same attitude and place."

"You ask if he wore a life-belt. Alas, no. They were too scarce. ..."
As one of the surviving stewards has stated that he helped Mr. Stead to fasten on his life-belt, it is very clear that our Chief made yet one more sacrifice, his last. ...

"Greater love hath no man."

Since that dark night there have been "Stead" messages innumerable, in which we, his friends, have been anxious to find some trace of his still living personality. We apply to them his own test, that of internal evidence, the final test. "It is the substance of a message that makes its value," he used to say. Even so, we believe he has appeared visibly and spoken audibly to many of us; and has conveyed his thoughts by writing and by impression, this last the swiftest

---

[49] The names of "that brave little orchestra" are: W. Hartley (leader), P. C. Taylor, J. L. Hume, G. Krins, W. Woodward, W.T. Brailey. The last-named is the son of Mr, R. Brailey, a well-known London psychic.

and most delicate of all forms of intercommunion between spirit incarnate and discarnate.

I do not attempt to dogmatize as to the genuineness of psychic communications which may sometimes seem to contradict each other. Perhaps even such seeming contradictions might be reconciled if we really understood the difficulties under which they have been conveyed.

That we of Julia's Circle feel we have had incontrovertible evidence that W.T. Stead still lives and works, enough has already been published elsewhere to show. I need not therefore go over that ground again. His daughter was amongst the first to place her testimony on record.[50]

Yet to meet the possible objection that many of these communications have come through persons who had known him intimately, I am tempted to emphasize one of the earliest, the experience of Lady Archibald Campbell, who had met him but once. Her message is in essence the same, though clothed in different words, as many other communications, judged authentic, which came at the time through several different channels within a week of the disaster. Those understanding something of the "science" of spirit manifestation so far as it is understandable realize that thought is the language of the spirit world, and that it takes form in such word-garments as are available from the recipient's mentality, as a strain of music is differently accentuated according to whether it is expressed through organ, violin, orchestra, or the human voice. At the time of the loss of the *Titanic*, Lady Archibald was staying at a remote country place by the sea, surrounded by all the psychic influences of the sea. She had had no news beyond the first conflicting tidings of horror published in the press: absolutely no details as to lost or saved. Two nights after the great vessel had gone down, clearly and distinctly, with the keen awareness of the "inner senses of the soul" the Highland birthright she heard the words: "W.T. Stead drowned!"

She then had a vision of the ship, seeming to feel herself actually upon it, experiencing with a sense of sudden shock a repercussion or echo, as it were, of the moment when the mighty leviathan rose up, like a "gigantic black wall" between sky and ocean, ere it sank like a

---

[50] See *Nash's Magazine* for June 1912: *My Father and Spiritualism*, by Estelle W. Stead; *The Voices*, by Vice- Admiral W. Usborne Moore; "Has W.T. Stead Returned?" by James Coates; an article by Major-General Sir A. E. Turner, in the *London Magazine*, December 1913; and "The Return of Mr. Stead," by the present writer, in The *Harbinger of Light*, February 1914.

stone into the deep. To her clairaudient ear came fitfully these words, the "influence" being unmistakably that of W.T. Stead,—

> "There is at present nothing no way to mark or show to survivors our varied experiences. To the rumour of waves, without recording apparatus, to the bottom of the sea went lost souls, for lost they were with despair coming in when hope was gone. ... Survivors there were who forgot the Divine law in saving themselves. ... I saw men and women lining the waters. It is difficult to picture to you how those people, balanced there, half-paralysed, remained with thoughts asleep while yet unknowing of their re-birth. I do not come back to prose about what happened, which cannot be undone, but to give light to the strong, partly to implore those left on earth to subscribe prayers and messages of love to those who went under the waves. I am weary as with the pressure of all the ends of the earth upon me. But I will employ my vigilance as long as it is diplomatic for me to be upon this earth. ... I have much to do. ..."

In granting me permission[51] to quote the foregoing lines Lady Archibald Campbell wrote:

> "MY DEAR MISS HARPER,—
> "I am very glad that in your recollections of Mr. Stead you intend alluding to my script, and that you care to have my first impressions of his personality, after the one and only occasion when I was privileged to meet him, as an earth-man. It was at a friend's house, a few months previous to the going down of the *Titanic*. Our talk was of course on mystic things, which, lasting one or two hours, passed for me as so many minutes. A brilliant, charming man, a radiating, prepossessing influence, because everything about him rang true! On referring to the prefatory remarks in my script I can say my first impressions of his personality abided with me. I had never seen eyes which showed more clearly the meaning of that expression 'the windows of the soul.' Through his windows his intense Ego wistfully seemed to look out at life's heavy riddle. Were they the eyes of a pilot, 'eyes dim with gazing on the pilot stars'? The idea struck me forcibly at the time, before his escaped soul, returning, confirmed it."

---

[51] I am also indebted to the editor of the *Occult Review* for his sanction. Lady A. Campbell's paper, "Through the Depths," appeared in that magazine in July 1912.

Among the letters that poured in from all parts of the world came one from Mrs. Annie Besant, one of Mr. Stead's oldest and most attached friends, who wrote from Italy:

> "It is hard to realize that the world has been deprived of so invaluable a worker, leaving a place which no one else can fill: always ready to speak for the truth, the right, never thinking of his own interests the rarest combination, and we need such men so badly. But I think he will return very soon, to take up his work and carry it on. Meanwhile, every good cause is the poorer and the weaker for his going."

This and such as this is the burden of every letter that came, to his home, his office, his friends. There were messages of heart-warm sympathy from Queen Alexandra; from Prince Omar Toussoun and the Egyptian Committee; from the Premier of Bulgaria; from Finnish journalists; from the Committee and Convention of the "Men and Religion Forward Movement," United States of America; from the Gaekwar of Baroda, from hosts of friends and admirers in South Africa, Australia, and the farthest Southern lands.

"My whole country loved Mr. Stead," said a Hindu gentleman to me; "his name is honoured in all the length and breadth of my land. We call him 'The Friend of India.'" It seemed as though his death had wakened a glow of passionate warmth all over the world, and persons who had never met, who will never meet face to face, clasped "hands across the sea" for the sake of Stead, the Man, who in death as in life seemed to belong to all. He worked for mankind and mankind paid its tribute [gladly, in wreaths of imperishable laurel, in the "loving thoughts that are as the life-blood of humanity, pulsing throughout the world."

One felt it everywhere; in the Memorial Service at Westminster,[52] when hundreds of voices joined in the singing of Cowper's old hymn "Begone, Unbelief!" chosen because Mr. Stead loved it for old time's sake;[53] more still one felt it in the thrilling organ-music at the close,

---

[52] Westminster Chapel, Buckingham Gate, April 25,. 1912.

[53] "The hymn that helped me most can lay no claim to preeminent merit as poetry. It is Newton's hymn which begins 'Begone, Unbelief.' I can remember my mother singing it when I was a tiny boy. To this day, whenever I am in doleful dumps and the stars in their courses appear to be fighting against me, that one doggerel verse comes back, clear as a blackbird's note through

when, not the Dead March in Saul, but the Hallelujah Chorus—pealed forth as the crowds streamed out of the great building into the outer air. The Memorial service left one cold, it made one think of death and the grave, and seemed to send him far away. But the glorious paean of joy in the Hallelujah Chorus that was our Chief indeed. One could breathe again.

What was the secret of this wonderful influence which he had over individuals and nations alike, which made it possible for his contemporaries to say, with deliberate judgment, that "he moulded the England of his day to a larger degree than any man in it"? His old friend of thirty years, Lord Fisher, gives the answer: "First and foremost, he feared God, and he feared none else. He was, indeed, *a human Dreadnought*. And next, he had an impregnable belief that *Right is Might*, and *not the other way round!"*

But there was still another reason, it lay in his deep and consummate knowledge of the human heart, which came to him through his intense power of loving, through his acutely-sensitive sympathy, which made him one in spirit with the friends and the causes he held dear.

"Human Dreadnought" though he was, yet the model and pattern on which he moulded his whole life day by day was Christ the divine Redeemer, the Master, on whose breast he leaned, and whose heart-throbs he felt in all the sorrows of the world. In the Passion of Christ for mankind he beheld the supreme ideal of all love.

In his old paper, the *Pall Mall Gazette*, it is written:[54]

> "For the best part of forty years Stead interpreted his Age with a clear and restless eloquence which had no superior and hardly a rival in his own profession of journalism. Statesmen and autocrats came under his spell and suffered him to prompt them when they would hardly brook advice from their appointed Ministers. This deference went far to nurse an obsession in the man which would have made him the most consummate egotist of our time, *had it not been for his sense of a superhuman mission*. It kept him a visionary to the end, and thus one of the most modern of men was one in spirit with the zealots of the Middle Ages. *Time is showing that his motives were sound at*

---

the morning mist. The verse, "as it is, with all its shortcomings, has been as a lifebuoy, keeping my head above the waves when the sea raged and was tempestuous, and when all else failed." W.T. Stead, in *Hymns that have Helped*.

[54] 25th September, 1913.

*the core,*55[55] however they radiated into action and surprise. He was perhaps the most remarkable union of mysticism and politics we can show since Cromwell. ... And, to use a Cromwellian phrase, no one but himself could ever prevail upon Stead to consider himself mistaken."

Yes, this sense of a "superhuman mission" was the pole-star by which he steered his course. I have borrowed the phrase, yet I know he would shake his head. He so often said: "I am only trying to do the bit of work the Senior Partner has given me. He has some work for every one of us: the thing is, just to learn exactly what that is, and set about doing it. Nothing 'superhuman' in that!"

This work of his was threefold. He called it, Peace, Woman, Spirit,— terms for him synonymous, in their deepest meaning, with Love, Life, and Light. In the name of the first, long years ago, he forced England to remodel her Navy, for: "On the strength of the British Navy rests the peace of the whole world"; and that strength is "Two Keels to One." In the name of Peace for he believed in the "civilizing Sovereignty of a great Power"—he preached his invincible gospel of Imperialism, the Imperialism of Responsibility—by which England makes herself answerable for peace, freedom and justice in all lands over which the flag of Britain waves. "His work for the Navy," writes Mr. J. L. Garvin, his successor in the famous editorial chair of the *Pall Mall Gazette*, "was the work of a statesman, full of the true vision of patriotism; and it would have been enough of itself to ensure memory for any career, and to keep that memory high." Cecil Rhodes once said:

"Stead is the greatest patriot I know. England is his home, and every foot of ground over which the British flag flies is his native land."

In the name of Woman he faced obloquy and persecution, and won his proud guerdon of prison garb and cell—for the sake of the little ones, than to offend whom "it were better that a millstone were hanged round a man's neck and he were cast into the sea." His lofty and pure nature held in ideal reverence the supreme sacrament and consecration of the love of man and woman as ever typical of the union of God and the soul. "Certainly women never had a braver knight," said Dr. Clifford. "All women in all lands were his care; but chiefly women suffering, crushed by the tyrannies of men. No movement that gave promise of help to women called in vain for his sympathy and devotion."

---

[55] Italics mine. E. K. H.

Loyola and the warrior-saints of old placed the deathless passion of their dreams on the Madonna. But he, the knight crusader of today, was "in love with the Woman-Soul of the World," and guarded his ideal, as with flaming sword Michael guarded the gate of Paradise.

And in the name of Spirit—the three-in-one—he waged his ceaseless warfare on materialism, and proclaimed his glad tidings of Life eternal and Love for evermore.

Some Dates in The Life of William Thomas Stead

~

1849.—July 5th.—Born of the Rev. William Stead and Isabella Stead at Embleton Manse, Northumberland.

The family removed to Howdon-on-Tyne, where his father was for thirty-four years pastor of the Congregational Church.

1861.—Went to Silcoates School for the sons of Congregational ministers and others, for two years.

1863.—Went as office-boy into the office of Mr. T. Y. Strachan, accountant, Newcastle-on-Tyne.

Engaged as clerk by a firm which was also the Russian Vice-Consulate for Newcastle-on-Tyne.

Wrote several essays for prize competition in the *Boys' Own Magazine*. The first was on "Coal"; the second on "The Villains of Shakespeare"; the third (which gained a prize) on "Oliver Cromwell."

His reading and writing were arrested for a time by weakness in the eyes. He made only slow progress, by having others to read to him. He took this as sign that he must devote himself more to the affairs of the village, and especially to the lads in his Sunday-school class. This he did. He also busied himself for the improvement of roads and better sanitation in the village. His eyesight gradually recovered.

The office where he was clerk being visited by numbers of beggars, he began writing letters in the *Northern Daily Express*, advocating the formation of a Mendicity Society for inquiry into alleged cases of distress, and so preventing fraud. As someone afterwards said, "He mounted to fame on a beggar's back."

Then began to write for the *Northern Echo*, a halfpenny daily just established in Darlington.

1871.—Became Editor of the *Northern Echo*, on the invitation of John Hyslop Bell (for the proprietors).

1873.—June 14th. Married Emma Lucy, daughter of Henry Wilson, of Howdon-on-Tyne, and took up his abode at Oaklands, or Grainey Hill, in the outskirts of Darlington.

1876—Was moved by letter of MacGahan in the *Daily News*, describing the atrocities practised by the Turks upon the Bulgarians at Batak, to take a leading part in the agitation which followed.

1877—First met Madame Novikoff, Mr. Gladstone, Thomas Carlyle.

1880.—Published *Electors' Catechism*.

Became Assistant Editor to John Morley at the *Pall Mall Gazette*.

1882—Published *Fifty Years of the House of Lords*.

1883.—Published *England, Gordon, and the Soudan*.

Became sole Editor of the *Pall Mall Gazette*.

1884.—Interviewed General Gordon, which led to Gordon being sent to Khartoum.

Organized Commission of Inquiry into Conditions of the Poor along the lines followed two years after by Mr.—Charles Booth.

Published *Who is to Have the Soudan?*

Secured by circular a majority of Liberal M.P.'s to declare for the retention of Irish Members at Westminster; "government by circular."

Published *The Truth About the Navy*.

1885.—Opposed by articles and pamphlets the idea of war with Russia over the Penjdeh incident.

Published *Too Late, Fight or Arbitrate* and *The Navy of Old England*.

Published The Maiden Tribute of Modern Babylon.

Spoke at many meetings on the subject of his approaching trial.

September.—Tried at Bow Street along with Bramwell Booth, Sampson Jacques, Mrs. Coombes, and Mrs. Jarrett.

November 4th.—Was sentenced to three months' imprisonment, and edited the *Pall Mall Gazette* in prison.

1886.—Published *No Reduction, No Rent!* (Plan of Campaign), *Deliverance or Doom, John Morley: the Irish Record of the New Chief Secretary*, and *Lord Randolph Churchill: Radical or Renegade?*

1887.—Took up the Langworthy case.

Published *Remember Trafalgar Square!* and *Not for Joe!*

1888.—Visited Russia; was received by Tsar Alexander III.

Published *The Truth About Russia.*

Attended Parnell Commission.

1889.—Visited Rome, and (next year) published *The Pope and the New Era and Pigottism and the "Times."*

1890.—Left the *Pall Mall Gazette* and founded the *Review of Reviews.*

Published *Portraits and Autographs.*

Witnessed the Passion Play at Oberammergau, and published *The Story that Transformed the World*, and *The Passion Play as Played To-day.*

Published *Discrowned King of Ireland.*

1891.—Issued *Help* (Feb. 1891–Dec. 1892).

Founded *American Review of Reviews.*

Published *Character Sketches* and *Real Ghost Stones.*

1892.—Founded *Australasian Review of Reviews.*

Published *More Ghost Stories.*

Published *The Electors' Guide* (L.C.C. Election) and *On the Eve* (Handbook to the General Election).

Began automatic writing.

1893.—Founded *Borderland*, which ceased in 1897.

Visited America and the Chicago World's Fair.

Wrote *Two and Two Make Four*, and included in it an attempt to float the Daily Paper, Limited, with a capital from subscriptions paid a year in advance.

1894.—Published *Christ Came to Chicago*.

Published *The Labour War in the United States* and *Fifty Years of the House of Lords*, 2nd edition.

Got up national memorial for arresting the growth of European armaments by international agreement.

Published *The Splendid Paupers*.

1895.—Started *Books for the Bairns* and Masterpiece Libraries of Penny Poets, Novels, and Prose Classics.

Published *Blastus, the King's Chamberlain*.

1896.—Held meetings in favour of arbitration on the Venezuelan question.

Published *Always Arbitrate Before You Fight*.

Published *The History of the Mystery; or, the Skeleton in Blastus's Cupboard*.

Published *Hymns That Have Helped*.

Founded the Scholars' International Correspondence.

1897.—Published character-sketch, *Her Majesty the Queen* and *Notables of Britain*.

Visited America.

Published *Satan's Invisible World: A Study of Despairing Democracy*, and *Letters from Julia*.

1898.—August 24th.—Tsar's Rescript.

Visited Russia; twice received by Nicholas II.

Published character-sketch, *Gladstone*.

Made a tour of Europe, visiting most of the capitals in favour of the Tsar's scheme for Peace.

1898-9.—Conducted series of meetings in support of The Hague Conference.

1899.—Published and edited a weekly paper, entitled *War Against War.*

Published *The United States of Europe.*

Went to Russia to present signatures of the Memorial to the Tsar.

From St. Petersburg went to The Hague; remained during the whole of the Conference.

Outbreak of South African War, which he strongly opposed.

Published weekly for nine months the organ, *War Against War in South Africa* (Oct. 1899–Aug. 1900).

Published *Shall I Slay My Brother Boer? Are We in the Right? The Scandal of the South African Committee*, and *Shall We Let Hell Loose in South Africa?*

1900.—Visited Oberammergau to witness the Passion Play, and wrote *The Crucifixion.*

In Paris during the Exhibition working for the cause of Internationalism.

Published *Mr. Carnegie's Conundrum* and *Mrs. Booth: A Study.*

Published *The Candidates of Cain* and *How Not to Make Peace.*

Published *Pen Pictures of the War by Men at the Front.*

Published *Lest We Forget.*

1901.—Published Stories of the Queen and *Methods of Barbarism.*

1902.—Published *The Conference of The Hague, The Americanization of the World, The Last Will and Testament of Cecil John Rhodes* and *The Despised Sex.*

Advocated the study of Esperanto in the *Review of Reviews.*

1903.—Published *How Britain Goes to War.*

1904.—Founded the short-lived *Daily Paper.*

Went to South Africa and began an active propaganda among the Boers in favour of peace and reconciliation.

September.—Went to his first play.

Published *Here Am I, Send Me* and *Are There Any Free Churches?*

1904-5.—Published pamphlets on the Revival in Wales.

1905.—Visited Russia; saw the Emperor and addressed meetings throughout the country pleading for the acceptance of the Duma.

Published Which? *Christ or Cain.*

1906.—Organized visit of German editors to this country.

Published *Tales and Talks of Tolstoy.*

Published *The Best or the Worst of Empires, Which? The Electors' Guide and The Liberal Ministry of 1906.*

1907.—Published *Peers or People.*

Visited the various European capitals, setting forth the idea of the Peace Budget and the Peace Pilgrimage.

Visited America to attend Peace Congress in New York; on returning from America paid return visit of English editors to Germany.

From Germany went to The Hague, and produced every day at his own expense a paper entitled *Courrier de la Conference.*

1909.—Published *The M.P. for Russia* (two vols.).

Julia's Bureau Founded.

1910.—Went to Oberammergau.

Gave evidence at the Divorce Commission.

1911.—Visited Constantinople on a mission of Peace.

Published *Tripoli and the Treaties.*

1912.—Easter Week. Sailed from Southampton for New York on the *Titanic* to address the Men and Religions Congress on "Universal Peace." The *Titanic* struck an iceberg late on the night of 14 th April, and sank in mid-ocean in the early hours of Monday, April 15th. Upwards of 1,600 persons sank with her, among them being W. T. Stead.

Appendix

M R. STEAD, AT THE TIME of publishing the autoscript referred to in Chapter 9, p. [insert], submitted it to several critics, including Sir Oliver Lodge, all of whom failed to find the junction of the two parts. Since then, however, and while revising the proofs of this book, I showed the message to Sir Oliver, and this time he was successful in finding the "join.' At Sir Oliver's suggestion, for the benefit of readers who may have been unable to detect where one script ends and the other begins, I append the explanation that Mr. Stead's concludes with the words "The main army," and mine begins with the words "The pioneers."

***

I regret that by an oversight an error on page [insert] has remained uncorrected. Madame Novikoff is there referred to as "god-daughter of the Tsar Nicolas II." It should of course be Nicolas I. Nicolas I, Emperor of Russia, 1825-1855, was a grandson of Catherine the Great.

www.ingramcontent.com/pod-product-compliance
Lightning Source LLC
Chambersburg PA
CBHW030827090426
42737CB00009B/901